WHAT IS TRUTH

CHRISTIAN D. LARSON

2015 by Neo Editions (NEOEDITORIALBOOKS@GMAIL.COM). This book is a classic, and a product of its time. It does not reflect the same views on race, gender, sexuality, ethnicity, and interpersonal relations as it would if it was written today.

CONTENTS

ABOUT THIS BOOK

THE greatest question before the mind of man always has been, and always will be, WHAT IS TRUTH?

It is a theme, therefore, that is always new—a theme that ever holds the deepest of interest for all who desire to know. And every book that deals with this theme in a broad, comprehensive, original manner will be more than welcome everywhere. And we claim that this is such a book. We also claim that all who read this book will not only gain a larger, a higher and a more interior conception of truth, but will, in addition, secure that finer vision of real truth that mankind in general has never been able to discern.

FOREWORD.

To formulate a complete and final definition for truth is not possible, the reason being that the truth in itself, or in any of its expressions, cannot be circumscribed by the human mind. The truth is too large to be described by any definition, however basic or comprehensive it may be. The best we can do, therefore, is to define our highest conceptions of truth. And moreover, we shall find this to be sufficient.

To define and understand our highest conception of truth is to know, in the present, as much of the truth as we shall find necessary to gain that freedom that invariably comes with the truth. And as we continue to seek higher and higher conceptions of truth, as we advance in life, we shall accordingly find that greater measure of freedom which must necessarily accompany the more advanced stages of human existence.

The purpose, therefore, of this book is not to present a clear-cut definition of truth, nor to give an answer to the question: What is truth? that would stand the test of all thought and experience. No, indeed, for such a course would defeat the aim we all have in view—the finding of more and more truth, and would make the search of truth far more difficult. The reason for this will be evident as we peruse the following pages.

Our purpose in this work is rather to present a plan or outline by which any individual may guide his mind in the attainment of higher and higher conceptions of truth in all its phases, and thereby understand the truth for himself at every stage of advancement which he may reach in his own sphere of life, thought and action. And this is the only rational course to pursue, for each individual must understand the truth for himself if he is to know that truth that brings freedom; but in order that he may understand the truth for himself he must seek and find the truth for himself. The only truth that is of any value to us is that truth that we have gained through our own individual efforts to actually know truth and inwardly realize the presence and power of truth.

This being true, all wide-awake and progressive minds will agree that the aim of this book, which is to present practical and effective methods through which anyone may find more and more truth, instead of trying to give a final and complete system of thought supposed to contain all the truth, which is impossible—all such minds will agree that this aim is the only aim, in this connection, that can possibly be rational in its process and practical in its application. And it is for such minds that this book is written. We feel, therefore, that every page will be fully appreciated, and that every statement will be thoroughly understood.

1

THE MEANING OF TRUTH.

No aim can be higher than that of seeking truth, and no reward can be greater than that of finding the truth. In fact, it is now considered by everybody that the greatest virtue of all virtues is to have an intense and ceaseless desire for truth. And the greatest good of all that is good is to realize a greater and greater measure of real truth.

The necessities of life are many, but there is nothing that man needs so much as more truth. To possess the truth is to possess everything that we can use now, and also to possess the key to everything that we may require for the future. The great objects of every normal person are invariably emancipation and attainment. To be set free from the imperfect and the lesser and to attain the perfect and the greater—this is what everybody is consciously or unconsciously working for; and truth can accomplish this, but truth alone. 'To know the truth is to secure complete emancipation; and to know the truth is to ascend into higher and higher attainments.

The awakened minds of every age have realized that the knowing of truth was the one great secret that could unravel all other secrets; and they have given their lives trying to reveal to mankind what truth really might be. Nevertheless, the race does not know, and the universal question still continues to be, What is truth? To answer this question, however, is not difficult, but it is difficult for most minds to comprehend the answer. The human mind too often believes its own conception of a truth to be the truth itself, and here is where the difficulty lies. This is the one great mistake of every age. Truth is one thing, but man's conception of truth is quite another thing.' Truth is eternal, unchangeable and complete, while man's conception of truth is temporal, mutable, and incomplete. To absolute truth nothing can be added, nothing taken away, but man's conception of truth is frequently wrong, even when it may appear to be absolutely right.

The truth is infinite and immeasurable. No one, therefore, can know the whole truth. To claim that you have found the absolute truth, or that you have discovered the perfect path to absolute truth is, in consequence, to delude yourself. The truth is so large that no one can ever find it all. We may devote an eternity to the finding of more and more truth, and yet, what we have found is insignificant compared to the immensity of the whole truth itself. The truth is everywhere, therefore there is no one perfect path to the truth. Every mind is in the truth, literally filled and surrounded by the truth, but no mind can contain the whole truth. It is possible to discern truth and know truth, but it is not possible to actually comprehend the truth. It is possible to understand the mental conception of truth, but it is not possible to understand truth itself.

The truth may be defined as an eternal state of perfect being; therefore, to know truth is to know that real being is perfect, and also that the perfect state of real being is eternal. To obtain a larger and a larger mental conception of eternal perfection of real being, or fundamental reality, is to grow in the truth. To grow in the truth is to find more truth, and to pass into the larger, the better, and the superior.

To accept a mental conception of truth as the truth itself is to bring all growth to a standstill, but this is what mankind in general has been doing and is doing. And because of this the majority remain in mental darkness, bondage and inferiority. An age that worships someone mind's conception of truth invariably becomes materialistic, no matter how lofty that mind was that originally formed the conception of truth that is worshiped. A materialistic mind is a mind that lives in the effects of previous efforts and that does nothing to rise above such conditions as heredity has handed down.

Growth, however, comes from the breaking of bounds, from the leaving of the lesser and perpetually pressing on toward the greater. The materialistic mind is like the stagnant pool; it is inactive or practically dead, no matter how active or beautiful its surroundings may be. At the present time we find materialistic minds everywhere surrounded by the highest culture and the most beautiful in art, and on account of those surroundings we fail to discern the uselessness, and in many instances the detriment, of the materialism thus hidden from view. We may believe the stagnant pool to be a pond of living water, because it is found in a garden of roses. In like manner we may believe that minds found in the midst of art, learning and culture must surely be living, growing, aspiring minds; but when we draw very near in either case we are disillusioned. In this age the most detrimental form of materialism is practically hidden within circles of enchanting music, fascinating rituals, elegant rhetoric and royal garments. Accordingly, materialism itself is not discerned by the many, and they follow blindly, continuing in sickness, sin, and death.

Truth alone can give emancipation, but we cannot find the truth so long as we humbly worship what someone has said about the truth. In this age many efforts have been made to formulate the truth in some definite system, but how can we place that something into system that is infinitely larger than all systems? To follow a system of thought is to worship some mind's conception of truth and to ignore the real truth itself. A system, however, may be employed if it is employed solely as the means to higher conceptions, but as soon as we look upon a system as authority, our eyes will not be able to see the truth anymore.

Systems of thought, as well as systems of action, are necessary as a means to higher ends, but the higher ends will not be reached unless we constantly look through the system and keep the eye single upon the infinite, unchangeable and immeasurable truth. When using systems in this manner, however, we must remember that it is not possible to know absolutely any part of the truth upon which our mental eye may be directed. It is not possible, even for a mind that is ever becoming larger and larger, to comprehend the limitless at any time. All that we can do now is to form the largest and highest conception of truth that our present mental capacity can permit, and then proceed to enlarge that conception perpetually.

True wisdom comes through mental ascension into the unbounded truth, and not through a studied belief of what we now accept as the truth. That knowledge that has power is gained through the constant enlargement of mentality; that is, through the expansion of consciousness as the mind grows in the truth, and not from the accumulation of relative facts. Emancipation comes through ascension, and in no other way; that is, the ascension of the mind into a larger, a higher and a finer understanding of the truth. The mind that is perpetually passing into the greater is constantly being emancipated from the lesser. And the mind that is forever growing better is daily being set free from the ills of error and imperfection.

In this connection it is important to realize that the only cause of bondage is found in a settled or inactive condition of mind. There are many minds that think they have secured freedom through the acceptance of a certain system of thought, but the freedom they have received did not come from the system of thought itself. Freedom never comes from the acceptance of systems, but from the mind's ascension into the new and the larger. If a certain system leads you away from the imperfection of your present life you will be emancipated from that imperfection, but if you give the system the credit, you will worship the system. You will dwell in the mental conceptions upon which that system is based and your mind will not move any further toward the realization of larger truth.

In this very place millions have brought their lives to a standstill; they having accepted various new systems as the whole truth discovered at last, and they have settled down in that belief. When they first accepted the new system of thought their minds naturally gained a higher place, and they were set free to that extent; but when they began to worship the system as the great emancipator it ceased to be a means to higher things, and became a prison which they dared not leave lest they fall back into their former condition. A new system of thought if worshiped as the truth will prevent you from ascending further into truth, and will, therefore, in due course of time make your mind just as materialistic and as limited as it was in the past.

The fact that you have health, peace and contentment does not prove that you have found absolute freedom, or that you have realized absolute truth. There are thousands who have health, peace and freedom who do not follow any system of thought at all, and who do not claim to have found a single absolute fact. For here we should remember that whenever we accept a new system of thought our minds are changed in a measure, and a change of mind always tends to eliminate adverse conditions of the system, both physical and mental.

Our great purpose, however, is not simply to realize peace, health and attainment, but also to develop our own individuality. And if we continue our individual development, health, peace and attainment, and all other blessings will follow.

This being true, we must not permit anything that will in any way hinder our fullest individual expression. But the fact is that there is nothing that hinders individual expression and the development of individuality more than the acceptance of a fixed system of thought as the absolute truth itself. No matter how well it may be with you in your present condition, physically, mentally or financially, if your belief makes you dependent upon any person, institution or outside authority, your individuality is being kept down. And instead of moving forward, as you may think, you are actually on the path to retrogression.

The experience of all ages proves this fact, and what has crippled individuality, or caused man to deteriorate in the past, can do so again. It is the evidence of history that every fixed system of |thought has made mental and spiritual dwarfs of "its most faithful followers. We all understand the reason why. No individual mind can know the truth through the understanding of some other mind; therefore each mind must not only be permitted, but encouraged, to develop its own individual capacity for knowing the truth, and nothing must stand in the way of the perpetual ascension of the soul into new conceptions of truth every day. The understanding of truth is promoted through individual research in all domains of life, and in the use of all the systems of thought available as means an end in the furthering of all research. It is therefore evident that individuality or the power of each mind to stand upon its own feet is indispensable in the search of truth. Fixed lines of action may be necessary in the systematic search for truth, but these lines should not be limited in number, nor confined to certain spheres of action.

Thousands of minds, otherwise intelligent, keep themselves in mental darkness because they refuse to seek truth outside of the usual lines. They forget that the lines now looked upon as usual and regular were once upon a time very unusual, and even considered dangerous. The fact is, however, that any line of research will lead to truth, and nothing is dangerous that will bring us more truth. We may therefore lay aside all fears, open wide all doors to all realms, and place our minds absolutely out in the open.

In the search of truth it is of the highest importance to be able to discriminate between truth itself and our mere mental conception of truth, and also between those conceptions that are true and those that are not. When you are dealing with a mental conception you are dealing with something that your mind contains, but when you are dealing with truth itself you are dealing with something: that contains your mind. A mental conception of truth is limited—it is something that mind can measure, but the truth itself is not limited, and therefore cannot be measured. False conceptions of truth, however, will not form themselves in your mind when you view the truth as infinite, and when the mind invariably ascends or tries to rise higher in the scale of understanding while attempting to realize more truth; in brief, a conception of truth is true as far as it goes if the mind expanded while that conception was formed. This is a simple rule and will be found to contain the greatest secret of all in the realization of more and more truth.

The fact is, that the aspiring or expanding attitude of the mind is the only attitude through which more truth can be gained, for no mental conception of truth is true unless it is superior to the conception that was formed before. And here it must be remembered that to know the truth is to know more truth. The very act of the mind in knowing the truth involves the act of knowing more truth at that particular time. Whenever the mind is trying to know the truth it must try to know more truth in order to know truth at all. We are not moving forward unless we are moving forward. For the same reason we are not knowing truth unless we are knowing more truth, because the truth is limitless, and every act of the mind that is attracted toward the knowing of truth must of necessity be attracted toward the knowing of all the truth. This means that every effort to know the truth must be a forward movement in the mind.

What was truth to you in the past is not truth to you now because that alone is truth to you now that you discern through your own present mental capacity, which is necessarily larger than your capacity was in the past. What we call truth is our present view of infinite truth, therefore if our present view is not superior to the past view we are still living in the past view; and if we are still living in the past view we are worshiping a system of outgrown beliefs; therefore do not see the truth at all.

The mental conceptions we form while in a stagnant state are not conceptions of truth; they are simply varying beliefs concerning the size and the structure of our prison walls; that is, the walls of the system in which we have incased ourselves. When you are confined in a system you are standing still, you see the bounds and the limitations of the system, but you do not see the boundlessness of the truth itself. And since we cannot form conceptions of truth unless we have our eyes directed upon infinite truth, the fact that your present conception is not superior to its predecessor proves that you are not viewing the truth. Accordingly, that conception cannot be true. The truth invariably lies in the line of an ascending scale of thought or mental action, while the untruth is formed when the mind is at a standstill, or is in the line of retrogression.

The understanding of truth is never fixed. A fixed understanding is no understanding, because to understand is to go deeper and deeper into the unfathomable states of the absolute; in brief, it involves an action of the mind. And any action of the mind that aims to understand must necessarily move toward the greater truth. We therefore see how impossible it is for any form of understanding to be fixed and stable. Comprehension does not comprehend unless it perpetually enlarges itself, because when the mind ceases to expand it ceases to act, and when it ceases to act no comprehension can take place. To comprehend is to go around, but if we are not going there necessarily will be no comprehension.

We therefore realize how necessary it is that every effort to know truth must be an effort to comprehend greater truth. The mind either goes out into the larger or remains at a standstill, though frequently when it remains at a standstill it is actually being contracted into a smaller mental sphere. When the mind remains at a standstill, or deteriorates, it does not act upon anything that is larger or superior to its past belief; and consequently the act of comprehension does not take place.

A mind that is belittling itself is not on the way to the realization of greater wisdom. The mind can know only through the act of ascension or expansion; that is, the rising in the scale of thought, feeling and consciousness. When the mind ceases to ascend it ceases to know, because the act of knowing is a forward movement of those mental processes that are involved in thinking, reasoning and similar acts of the mind. Therefore, when the mind ceases to ascend it begins to dwell in mental darkness, and from mental darkness come all the ills of life. To find the truth and to know the truth it is necessary to view the truth as infinite and immeasurable, and to ascend perpetually to a larger and a larger consciousness of that infinite view of truth.

When you think of things as entities, and try to know the truth concerning them, it is always necessary to turn the attention upon the limitless truth that is back of appearances. We cannot gain the truth about anything unless the mind expands into the consciousness of the all that is contained in everything. And we cannot ascend in this way unless we direct our research into the vast realms that are beyond all appearances. There will always be a beyond, but the beyond of today should be the tangible and demonstrated realities of the days succeeding. What is hidden today should be proven fact tomorrow. This is possible when we search for the truth, not in the world of appearances, but in the wider realms just beyond present appearances.

But our object in seeking the truth is not simply to possess the truth—it is also to find greater means for growth, progress and ascension. Emancipation and attainment are the two great aims in real life, and both are the results of knowing the truth. To know the truth is to ascend perpetually into the infinite domains of truth, thus leaving behind the lesser and forever entering into the greater. In this way we pass out of and rise above everything that has served its purpose and enter constantly into the marvels and splendors still in store.

2

HOW TO KNOW THE TRUTH.

The discovery of the subconscious mind and its extraordinary powers over the outer mind and the body is turning new light on many subjects. And we can safely predict that the understanding of the subconscious will in the near future practically revolutionize all thought and all methods of mental, moral and spiritual training. The fact that you can impress anything upon the subconscious and that all such impressions will react as corresponding expressions, is creating the most profound attention among all progressive thinkers, not only because it opens to the mind an immense field of most fascinating study, but also because it explains hundreds of phenomena that have hitherto baffled all attempts at solution.

Among the many mysteries that are explained by subconscious study, few are of greater interest than that of the origin of ideas or what might be termed beliefs and convictions. Many a person asks himself daily why he believes what he does, and why he is convinced that certain things are true when he has no evidence. If our convictions always proved themselves to be true this matter might not attract much attention, but the fact that so many convictions sooner or later prove themselves to be untrue or mere illusions makes the subject one of more than passing importance. What we believed yesterday we frequently discard today, and what we believe today we are quite liable to discard tomorrow, possibly with a few exceptions. Nevertheless, while the beliefs of today remain, we are so thoroughly convinced that they are true that practically nothing can change our minds. In fact, our present beliefs sometimes have such a powerful hold upon our minds that we have absolutely no desire to think differently from what we do. And what is more, those very beliefs, as a rule, refuse to be examined. It is certainly mental bondage with a vengeance when a mind dare not examine the credentials of its own beliefs, and is so completely under the control of its own convictions that it is unable to question their genuineness or authority.

But what we want to know is what places the mind in such a condition, and also what might constitute the path to emancipation. These are great questions when we realize the fact that there are millions of minds that are more or less in such a condition. The subconscious mind, however, explains the mystery. Our convictions, that is, those things that we feel to be true, are in most instances mental expressions from the subconscious.

When these expressions are very strong they invariably color all views, desires, motives, feelings or intentions of the outer mind. Sometimes these convictions, or subconscious expressions, are so strong that even a liberal university education will have to obey and color its ideas accordingly. We frequently ask, "How can that well educated man believe as he does?" The fact is that he is compelled by his own subconscious convictions to believe as he does. Those convictions are so strong that they bend, twist and color his education so that the education itself is made a servant of mere belief, and is not infrequently compelled to use its power to prove the genuineness of that belief.

But in the face of these facts, how are we to know that truth is truth? How are we to distinguish between a real principle and an opinion which is simply the reaction of some idea or belief that was previously impressed upon our minds? How are we to determine when a law is a law and when it is simply the tendency of a strong expression from the subconscious? To know these things is highly important, because the truth is the cause of all that is good, while the untruth is the cause of all that is not good.

To distinguish truth from error we have usually depended upon logic, or upon scientific evidence, but a study of the subconscious proves that logic is not always safe, and also that scientific evidence may be so colored and modified as to prove the very opposite as to what happens to be fact. An expression from the subconscious, if very strong, can so modify the logical process that reason is literally compelled to act along certain lines only, and wholly ignore certain other lines which if considered would change the conclusion decidedly. We have any amount of this sort of reasoning going on all about us, and it is responsible for a great many false views as well as half-truths.

In addition to the twisting process, which is constantly applied to logic or reason by prejudice, strong personal feelings and contradicting subconscious convictions, there is another process originating wholly in the subconscious, which makes logic still more incompetent to prove that truth is truth. The logical process is based upon premises, and the conclusion is true only when the premises are true. If one or both of the premises are false, the conclusion will be false, even though the reasoning employed be absolutely sound in every respect.

The process of logical reasoning is similar to the working out of a mathematical problem. If one of the original figures were wrong, the final answer will be wrong, regardless of the fact that the process be entirely correct all the way through. In logic it is therefore necessary to have correct premises at the beginning, but how are we to know that they are correct? A strong, preconceived subconscious conviction may color or modify any premises which we may formulate, and make it appear true when it is false, or vice versa. What is more, a strong subconscious conviction may influence the mind to form all of its premises so as to harmonize with that conviction, thus forcing the logical process to prove that the subconscious conviction is true, even though it may be the most impossible illusion. A great deal of this is done; in fact, there are few minds that are absolutely free from it.

Again, a great many impressions concerning the nature of life in general, and this or that in particular, may establish themselves so firmly in the subconscious that they are accepted as absolute facts; and these may be employed as fundamentals in the formulating of principles, laws, premises, and so on. Upon these fundamentals we may construct an immense system of thought which may seem to be plausible, reasonable, and logical, and we may gain thousands of followers even though there may not be a single truth at the bottom of the system.

In this connection we must remember that any idea which seems plausible may impress itself upon the subconscious as a fact. And since we naturally accept what comes from the subconscious, provided the subconscious expression be very strong, we will believe this plausible idea to be a fact even though it may be nothing more than a mere illusion. It is the nature of the human mind to feel that whatever comes from the subconscious is true; that is, every expression from the subconscious feels as if it were real, and what we feel to be true or real we accept as final, usually asking no questions. But we must not blame the subconscious for such phenomena. The subconscious only responds to impressions from without. The conscious mind acts, the subconscious reacts, and the two actions are always similar.

When we accept an idea from another mind, or from our own study simply because it seems plausible, we will permit that idea to impress itself upon the subconscious, provided it is deeply felt. Later on that same idea will come back from the subconscious as a strong conviction; and we shall not only be forced to accept it as true, but in addition it will color all our thinking; in fact, it may become so strong that we do not care to be free from its absolute control. There are many illustrations of this very thing, as there are quite a number of people who are in such complete bondage to the mental control of the beliefs they cherish that they actually take pride in being under such absolute control; in brief, they frequently declare, "I am completely in the hands of this system of thought and I am glad of it."

The cause of this strange state of mind is easily explained, however. The absolute slave, be he physical or mental, does not wish to be free, because if he

IS an absolute slave he does not have sufficient freedom of thought to distinguish between bondage and emancipation; in brief, he cannot appreciate freedom. Therefore, it appears to him to be something that will deprive him of the privileges he may enjoy in his bondage. He would rather endure the present state, even if that state happens to be undesirable, than risk the uncertainty of that of which he has not the slightest conception.

There are a large number of minds in this condition; they are afraid to change their minds, because their bondage is so complete that they have not sufficient individuality or freedom of self-assertive-ness to stand upon their own feet should they be called upon to do so. They may be miserable where they are, but they are wholly unable to express a desire for change. They believe what they believe because that belief has become a deep-seated subconscious habit and their minds are completely under the control of those habits. Their habits of belief may have been formed in childhood under the strict discipline of "authority for truth"; or they may have changed later, accepting a new belief and permitting this new belief to sink so deeply into the subconscious that it colors all thought and prevents the mind from thinking anything which does not conform to this belief.

But the question is, if there need be any truth in a belief in order that it may gain such full control over the mind. That there may be some truth m all belief is possible, though from the nature of the case, the larger part of it will be untrue. We realize that any system, no matter how untrue, may gain complete supremacy in the mind and compel the mind to accept it as true. Therefore, the mere fact that our belief seems to be true proves nothing, nor does the fact that we are satisfied with our present belief prove anything in its favor.

Many a serf is satisfied to be next to nothing, and many a mind knows so little that it looks upon its ignorance as a virtue. In fact, it was only a few years ago that ignorance was considered a virtue among a large percentage of people. Those people, however, were not to blame; in fact, no one is directly to blame. Nevertheless, the fact that all these things exist in our very midst but adds importance to our subject.

The great question before us is, "How are we to know the truth; that is, how are we to know the truth when we see it?" Thus far there is only one way through which we may know the truth, and that is what is called "the scientific method." This method has been applied by students of the physical universe for half a century or more, and they have in that way made modern science a marvel. But the same method can be applied in any department of thought or research, and must, if we are to distinguish the truth from what is not truth.

The scientific method is based upon the principle of permitting truth to demonstrate itself; or in other words, acting upon the statement, "By their fruits ye shall know them." When we proceed according to this principle we find that truth always demonstrates itself when permitted to do so; and also, any belief which does not prove itself to be the truth, proves itself through the same process to be the untruth.

In this age, one of the reigning desires is to find the truth; in consequence, wide-awake minds may be seen in large numbers going here and there and everywhere in search of the precious jewel. But how many of them know what the jewel looks like? Are we sure that most of us have not passed it by thousands of times, thinking it was something else? It has been said that "All is not gold that glitters" but we can with equal propriety declare, that all is not truth that dazzles the mind with the colorings of plausibility, though the average truth seeker is entirely too prone to accept the plausible as truth without further evidence. The ideas thus accepted invariably become subconscious convictions of more or less power, and we have a repetition of the old process until the new belief becomes a habit and controls the mind as it was controlled by the habits of belief which went before.

Knowing that subconscious convictions can so dominate judgment and reason that the true may appear to be false, and vice versa, it is wholly unsafe to accept anything as true until we have seen the fruits. We should therefore demand that every idea demonstrate its genuineness before it is made a part of the mind. No idea should be permitted to impress itself upon the subconscious until it has proved itself to be true, because the subconscious is like a fertile field. Anything will grow there if you simply drop the seed.

"As a man thinketh in his heart so is he"; and the thought of the heart is invariably that thought which is rooted in the subconscious. The thoughts, ideas, desires and convictions which enter the subconscious will wholly determine what we are to do, think or become. Whatever enters the subconscious will express itself in the personality, and whatever we accept with implicit faith will enter the subconscious. Since ever seed that is sown in the subconscious will positively bear fruit after its kind, and since what we accept as true will enter the subconscious, we cannot be too cautious with respect to what we think of as the truth; and should therefore require all ideas to prove themselves before we receive them.

But here we may ask what we are to do with all those beliefs that the race has for ages looked upon as sacred? Will it be necessary to take all these beliefs out and demand that they demonstrate themselves through the scientific method to be absolutely true before we reinstate them in our minds? The answer is, this is the course we must take. All truth is sacred, and nothing is sacred unless it is the truths The fact that we think a certain belief to be sacred does not make it so, even though it has been held sacred for a thousand centuries. We can easily get into the habit of thinking the most ordinary illusion to be a sacred truth, and finally be completely controlled by that belief. If a belief is true it will produce the fruits of the truth, which means all good things for life here and now. And if so, it is sacred. But if it produces no fruits or produces results that are undesirable, it must be examined. It may simply be a habit of thought that poses as sacred truth, and we want to know. Truth is for us, and if there is any idea in our minds that has all these years deceived us, we want to get rid of it at once, no matter how sacred it may have appeared in the eyes of ignorance.

The fact that we have to discard a few of the old beliefs when we begin to search for the truth need not disturb us in the least. We shall not be left empty-handed. The truth is everywhere. There are millions of great truths all about us, above us, beneath us, within us, and we have the power to know them all; therefore, we are perfectly safe in changing our minds in a few respects when we find that such changes will be conducive to a much larger understanding of the truth. To eliminate the useless will give place for that which can add more richly to the welfare and the beauty of life.

Concerning the demonstration of truth we must remember that we are living in the great eternal now, and in consequence can take interest only in those ideas that deal with the present. We cannot demonstrate anything concerning the future; therefore it is a misuse of the mind to try. It is also wrong, for the same reason, to fill our minds with beliefs which deal solely with future states of existence. To understand the life that we are living now is the problem, and to live this present life in the truest and most beautiful sense possible is the purpose. To fulfill that purpose we must know the truth about present existence, and must live the present life according to that truth. I And here we should remember that to make the present good is to make the future better, because what is to happen in days to come will be the natural result of what we are doing now.

3
HOW TO SEEK THE TRUTH.

In this age thinkers are becoming numerous, and all thinkers are seekers of truth. At any rate they try to be, but they are not all successful in this respect, the reason being that the principle upon which all search of truth must be based is not clearly understood. To the majority truth is a something that can be received from some other mind; therefore it is sought from those who are supposed to know or who claim to know. And this is the real reason why there are so few who really understand the truth, or who are actually growing in that understanding.

In the strictest sense of the term truth cannot be taught. One mind cannot teach the truth to another mind. And in the same sense the truth cannot be learned. It can only be realized, and realization is a process that no two minds enter into exactly in the same way. Methods for finding the truth may be given by one mind to another, but each individual mind must employ such methods as his own present conception of truth, life and reality can apply.

We all occupy different positions in life. Therefore we all shall have to begin differently in taking any step forward. And if this step is taken in our own best way it will invariably be a forward step. In like manner, since we all have different conceptions of the real we must seek to perfect our own conceptions. We cannot enlarge upon something in our own mind that never existed in our own minds. Therefore we must develop our own view of truth in order to obtain a better understanding of truth.

Before you can take a step from a lower position to a higher you must have a lower position upon which to stand. And that lower position must be under your own feet, not under the feet of another. To obtain a larger realization of truth each individual mind must begin by unfolding the truth that he already perceives through his own present realization, no matter how crude or undeveloped that realization may be. He must enlarge upon that which he himself is in possession of. He must begin his development with his own present state of development, and not try to imitate the understanding, the realization or the process of growth in another.

No progress is possible so long as we try to see truth through the eyes of another, or try to imitate the understanding that a more advanced mind may possess. This very thing, however, nearly all seekers of truth are trying to do, and in consequence they do not succeed in knowing truth. To believe the truth is one

16

thing. To know the truth is quite another. The former is possible to anybody, but it is only the latter that makes man free.

The average beginner in search of truth believes that his own conception of truth is wholly wrong. At any rate, he is usually told so by those who imagine they have discovered the only truth; but in this respect they are quite mistaken. No conception of truth is wholly wrong. There is some truth in every belief that you may now entertain. Therefore begin with that tiny truth and continue to unfold it and enlarge upon it until it touches the universal on all sides. And when this process of growth is entered into you will find the way to perpetual growth in the absolute truth itself.

To develop the truth that may exist in your present conception of life and reality, the first essential is to open the mind on all sides. Realize that the truth is the soul of everything, and that something good can be gained from everything by opening the mind to this soul wherever it may be found.

Whenever a person declares that there is nothing in this or that, or that such and such is impossible, he places obstacles in the way of his own understanding, and therefore closes the door more or less to the truth. There positively is something in everything, and to find the truth about everything you must recognize this something in every phase of existence. This, however, is not possible so long as you continue to close your mind to everything that does not appeal to your understanding at first sight.

Everything that exists or that appears has some reality back of it or within it. Even so-called illusions are mental clouds that hide some light of truth. Therefore, instead of ignoring the mere appearance as worthless, the hidden truth that is certainly back of those things should be sought directly and with persistence. By tracing an illusion back to its origin you may make a great discovery. This very thing has been done a number of times. In fact, most of the greatest discoveries made in the world have been made exactly in this manner.

The man who refuses to investigate what does not appeal to him at first sight will never find real truth, nor will he become an original thinker. He will continue to remain a follower and will blindly believe what custom has made safe and respectable. To say that there is nothing in this or that is to close the mental door to that something that is there, thus depriving yourself of a truth that might be the very truth you are seeking now.

All truth is valuable and extremely important, but the truth that we actually need now is usually the truth that is hidden beneath the common misconceptions of everyday life. But we usually judge according to appearances and conclude that there is nothing in these things; therefore we fail to find what we want. Back of every truth there are scores of other truths and larger truths. It is therefore evident that when we close the mental door to those that are nearest we separate ourselves from a universe of rare wisdom.

To declare that this or that is impossible is to limit the power of truth, and when we place a limitation upon the power of truth we place a limitation upon our own power to understand truth. The mind that lives in the faith that all things are possible is the mind that opens itself more and more to the truth and that power from within that can make all things possible. In consequence such a mind develops daily in capacity, ability, understanding and power.

In this connection the proper course is to believe that there is something in everything, and to resolve to find it. Believe that everything is possible and resolve to prove it. Through this attitude your mind will expand in every direction, gaining light, wisdom and power from every source. To open the mind to truth on all sides is to bring consciousness into touch with an infinite sea of truth. The mind therefore will live perpetually in pure light, and will constantly gain a larger measure of this light.

Never say, "I do not believe this." You draw down one of the shades by so doing thereby excluding some of the sunlight of real truth. Say rather, "I believe the truth that is back of everything, therefore I respect everything, and will penetrate everything so as to find all the truth, and thus grow perpetually in the realization of all truth."

Do not attempt to gain truth by absorbing the views of others. On the other hand, do not attempt to gain truth by secluding yourself from the views of others. Proceed to develop in yourself the understanding of truth and you will find that the views of advancing minds will become nourishing food for that understanding. But so long as you have no real understanding of truth, or if your present conception of truth be undeveloped, the more advanced ideas you try to absorb the more confused you become.

When you have begun to understand the truth, that is, when you have begun to unfold your own present conception of the truth, you will find that every person, every book, every idea and every belief that you may come in contact with will prove to be an inspiration, and will help to open your mind to higher conceptions and deeper realizations.

In the search of truth we must remember that instructions from others are valuable only, in so far as we are able to interpret the inner meaning of the tangible facts presented. And this ability develops by our trying to feel and understand the soul of every idea that enters the mind. Knowledge becomes a power in us only when we feel within us the real soul of that knowledge.

The real truth seeker must try to interpret the meaning that underlies all phenomena, all experience, all events and all ideas. He must constantly keep the fact in mind that there is something back of everything. And he must seek this something in everything that is met in life. We shall find in this connection that the perpetual growth in truth will naturally follow the effort to realize the inner or soul existence in everything with which we may come in contact. Truth is found directly by seeking to understand the interior essence of life through one's own interpretations of life and through the development of one's own insight into principles, laws and things. In other words, when we enlarge our own present conception of truth we gain a larger interior conception of all truth as all truth appears from our present point of view.

With most minds too much time is given in trying to find truth in the outside world, and not enough time is given to the development of that power within us that alone can know the truth. To receive a message of truth from some great mind is not sufficient. You must try to understand the spirit, the life and the real soul of that message by entering mentally into the deepest conception of that message that you can possibly form in your own consciousness. Truth will not come to you through any message or form of instructions if you make no attempt to go beyond the literal statements.

It is the inner life of things that contains the truth. Therefore, to understand the truth you must develop that insight that can discern the interior, the seemingly hidden, or the very soul of existence. The great secret in finding truth is to enter more closely into harmony with the interior soul life of everything, thereby developing the higher consciousness that actually knows truth.

We should make it a point to listen to everyone who has a reasonable message; that is, a message that deals directly with truth, unsystematized truth; but we should learn to interpret that message through our own conception of truth. We should welcome the thoughts of others on all subjects, but we should not accept those thoughts as final statements. We should not take the literal meaning, but look for the inner meaning of every word that is spoken. We should analyze the thoughts of others, but do our own independent thinking. Though we must not imagine that we have begun our own thinking simply because we have discarded one system of belief and adopted another.

We should pay no attention to a message that deals simply with doctrines and opinions. It is life in all its manifestations that we wish to understand. And when we understand life we shall also understand everything that pertains to life, or that comes from life. A message of truth invariably deals with life and the living of life now. Therefore we can readily distinguish between what is claimed to be a message of truth and one that actually is a message of truth.

What we are thinking at the present time is very important, therefore every thought of the present should be created in the likeness of truth; but it is equally important that we move constantly into larger thought, superior thought and higher conceptions of true thought. A message that presents a fixed system of belief; that is, a belief supposed to contain the truth, is of no value to the truth seeker. To adopt a fixed system, no matter how good it may seem to be is to cease to be a seeker of truth.

To seek the truth is to seek constantly a larger and larger understanding of truth; that is, to enlarge upon one's present conception of truth and enter again and again into new truth. But neither new truths nor larger truths ever spring from a fixed system. To gain the understanding of larger truth and steadily grow into the absolute truth the mind must constantly expand. But the mind that adepts a fixed system will remain fixed, therefore cannot expand.

What the truth seeker wants is methods that promote individuality and originality, methods that lead the mind upward and onward in every direction. It is not something to believe that is wanted, but something that we can use in developing the mind so that we can understand the very foundation of all belief. We do not want ideas that will simply satisfy the intellect. We also want methods that will expand, enlarge and develop the intellect. We do not want a religion or a philosophy that we can accept as authority. We want a science of living that will so develop man that the man himself can speak as one having authority. Truth does not come through believing something. It comes through the use of that something that unfolds, develops and elevates the mind.

A great many truth seekers believe that it is necessary to work independently in order to promote originality of thought, and therefore they have a sort of fear of personalities, systems and institutions. But this is a mistake, because nothing can hold you in bondage unless you fear that bondage. On the other hand, all things may at times serve as means through which a higher conception of greater truth may be attained. And here we should remember that more mental bondage comes from the fear of institutions than from the institutions themselves. The real truth seeker is friendly to all minds, to all beliefs, to all systems and to all institutions, because he knows that back of them all there is some truth, and through friendly relations that truth may be found. He also knows that when we are friendly with all things all things will be with us, and what is with us will help us on to greater things.

This being true, we should eliminate the critical spirit and encourage the analytical spirit. In brief, we should try all things and hold fast to the good. The critical mind may have plausible opinions, but it is not possible to realize the truth while we are in critical or antagonistic states of mind. This is a fact of enormous importance, a fact that should be so deeply impressed upon every mind that it will never be forgotten. The mind that is looking for the truth that is back of all things will not criticize anything, because to such a mind all things are paths to greater truth and therefore to the greater goal we may have in view.

In our search of truth we must remember that it is not sufficient simply to seek the truth. We must also live the truth. If we fail to live the truth that we have found we will soon lose that truth, and also close the door to new truth. By living the truth that we now understand we open the mental door to more truth and larger truth, for the fact is that when we apply what we know we gain the power to know more. This is especially true when we live in the aspiring or the spiritual attitude. And we live in the spiritual attitude when our mind is open to the best from all sources.

As we proceed in the application of any particular principle, we shall so enlarge the mind that other and more important principles will be comprehended. The application of all of these in turn will expand consciousness still farther, and so on indefinitely, until a universe of wisdom is held in the grasp of the mind. To apply the truth in its present limited phases will develop the understanding of larger phases. Any mind, therefore, may begin with the most limited understanding of truth, and in the course of a few years have an understanding that cannot be measured.

Nothing should be accepted as truth that does not appeal to reason. The idea presented may be true, but if it does not appeal to your reason you cannot apply it now; and what you cannot apply is of no present use to you. However, do not criticize or condemn what you cannot accept. There is truth back of it because there is truth back of everything, even though you may not see it now. Therefore suspend judgment for the present and proceed to develop a finer insight and a finer mind so that you may in the future see what may be hidden in the present.

Although all truth must appeal to reason before it can be applied, reason must not be depended upon exclusively in finding the truth. It is the finer perceptions and insights that occupy the most important position in the discovery of truth. Therefore if you are a truth seeker proceed to develop those faculties by using them constantly wherever your attention may be directed.

If all these perceptions and insights were universally developed, we should all see the truth so clearly that there would be practically no disagreements concerning what is true and what is not true about this sphere of existence. However, our object must not be to try to agree, but to develop the power to understand the truth, for when this power is developed perfect agreement among us all will come of itself.

In the search of truth the imagination must be held under perfect control. The majority, however, among the truth seekers permit their imaginations to form all sorts of ideas and conceptions, and they frequently accept these as true, regardless of evidence. This is one reason why illusions and half-truths are so numerous.

Another essential is to keep the emotional nature in poise. Our emotions tend to excite the imagination, and a number of artificial ideas will be impressed upon the mind. Many of these will be so deeply impressed that they appear to be true, because when the mind is in an intense emotional state nearly every idea formed at the time will be deeply felt. And what is deeply felt we usually accept as the truth whether it is or no.

One of the greatest essentials in the search of truth is the spiritual viewpoint; that is, to examine all things from the principle that the soul or the reality that is back of all things is absolutely perfect and absolutely true. The purpose of life is perpetual growth in the realization of perfection. Therefore we must stand upon the principle of possible perfection in all things, and deal with all things according to that principle.

The understanding of truth does not mean the acceptance of a fixed idea that has proven itself to be true, but the perpetual unfoldment and enlargement of that idea through the constant growth of the mind in the realization of truth. The process of understanding is not a fixed attitude of mind, but a constant deepening and widening of mind as consciousness grows deeper and deeper into the very soul of reality, and expands in every direction toward the wider comprehension of reality.

You may think you understand the deep things of life, but there is still a larger universe beyond what you may understand. And to understand this the mind must constantly enlarge and deepen its understanding toward greater depths of truth and wisdom. Every idea that is found contains truth, or the possibility of some unfoldment of truth; therefore by entering the soul of every idea and enlarging the present conception of that soul the hidden truth will be found. In addition many paths to other truth will be revealed.

Higher truth is discovered through the higher consciousness; therefore to try to compel people to believe what is beyond their present state of consciousness is a violation of mental law. Instead, we should teach man to develop himself and he will gain the greater understanding of life. He will also through this higher development learn to seek truth, learn where to find truth and learn how to apply truth.

The real secret of the truth seeker is to begin with his present conception of truth and develop himself in mind and soul through the perpetual enlargement of that conception; in brief, develop your power to understand greater truth by using the truth you now understand. This will positively give you the power to understand more truth and higher truth, and this is the great purpose we have in view.

4

WHERE TO FIND THE TRUTH.

The search for truth is becoming more and more extensive, and the desire to know truth for the sake of knowing is increasing with remarkable rapidity. For the same reason the number of new systems of belief are also increasing in proportion, as it is the general opinion that it is only through special systems of thought that the truth can be found. And the supply along any line of desire is always equal to the demand.

But the demands of the human mind are not always properly placed. Therefore we find many minds who desire systems based upon the latest conceptions of truth instead of upon the truth itself. This state of affairs causes rivalry among the various systems, and the question with them becomes not how to find more truth and live more perfectly according to the truth we know, but instead, which system is correct and which one is not.

Opposing systems, however, cannot all be correct, but since the advocates of each system believe their own to be correct they finally come to the conclusion that their own is the only true system. This conclusion is perfectly natural, because if you believe your belief to be correct, all other beliefs that do not agree with your own must be incorrect from your point of view. You therefore feel perfectly justified in declaring your own belief to be the only one through which the truth may be found.

The average mind looks at things only from his own point of view. He has not enlarged his consciousness sufficiently to know how it feels to be on the other side, therefore has nothing but his own limited experience upon which to base judgment. Accordingly, he cannot be blamed for what he thinks about his own favorite ideas. Though we must remember that no matter how convinced he may feel as to the exactness of his own conclusions we must hot accept them until we have compared them with others and found them to be superior.

When we study the nature of the mind we find that the tendency of the average person to think that his system of belief is the only system through which the truth can be found, comes from the general tendency to worship systems of thought instead of the all truth that is back of every system. When

23

you know that all systems are but varying interpretations of one absolute truth you will never say that your own system constitutes the only field wherein truth may be found, because you will know that all minds, even the most ignorant, know some of the truth. If they did not they could not continue to exist.

The very fact that a person continues to live and continues to secure certain results in providing for the essentials of life, proves that he is possessed of a considerable portion of the truth. If a person had no truth everything that he had would be false at its foundation, which would make his own individual existence impossible. This is a fact that we must well remember.

Another fact equally important is that no person can secure results in any field of action unless he applies the truth in that field. An action based upon mere falseness can produce nothing. Such an action cannot even enable a man to walk across the floor. To walk at all you must apply certain laws correctly. And to apply any law correctly you must have a correct conception of that law, conscious or unconscious. And to have a correct conception of anything is to know the truth to that extent.

The true use of anything can alone produce results, and the true use of anything is the application of a certain phase of the truth that lies at the foundation of that particular thing. Our conception of such truth may be subconscious only, but it exists in our minds. We possess it, and when we apply it we have results.

There are a great many things that we do not understand objectively, but the fact that we use them successfully proves that certain parts of our minds know the underlying laws and can, at least to a degree, apply those laws. According to these facts we realize that everything that lives must necessarily be in contact with the truth somewhere. If it were not it would produce a misstep at every turn, and nothing can continue to exist that produces missteps or mistakes only.

The average person deplores the fact that he makes so many mistakes, but when we stop to consider how many things we do that are not mistakes we conclude that things are not so bad after all. We have formed the habit of taking special notice of our mistakes just as the press of the world records mostly what is not good or desirable, because such things are exceptional, therefore constitute news. / Normal and wholesome actions in the social world do not constitute news./ They are too numerous. /And being normal they can be found in every nook and corner in the world. It is the normal, that is, the right and the good, that constitutes the rule of action in the world. 'It is the abnormal, or the bad, that constitutes the exception.

A man may act like a gentleman sixty minutes out of the hour and we pay no attention to that fact. However, should he act contrary to the principle of right for one minute the fact would be noted by everybody. And if that particular act was striking it would be wired all over the world. In his case the good would be sixty times as large as the evil, nevertheless, it would be the latter only that would constitute news, being so exceptional.

In like manner we may, as individuals, act according to the truth as far as we see it, and every minute of the hour. And no one pays special attention to such an unbroken series of good acts, unless, of course, those acts should be very striking or extraordinary. However, the very moment we make a mistake attention is aroused at once. If we make many of them our attention is very much concerned because we know by experience, if not by insight, that when the abnormal outnumbers the normal the end is near at hand.

Since a person can bring physical existence to an end simply by causing the abnormal actions to become more numerous than the normal ones, we can readily understand that he could not exist at all if all of his actions were abnormal. In fact, conscious existence could not even have a beginning under such conditions, and organic life would not be possible for a second. A life where every act was a mistake would be absolute chaos, and a state of absolute chaos is nothing. /Therefore, so long as a person lives at all it is evident that his normal actions are more numerous that his mistakes.

And a normal action is always a right action. A right action is the application of a truth in one or more of its phases, because nothing can be right unless it is based upon the truth. This proves that every existing entity knows consciously or unconsciously certain portions of the truth; And that therefore there can possibly be no one system through which all truth may be found, y

The problem that confronts us all, however, is how to so relate ourselves to the all truth about us, that we may find as much truth as we may need now in order to make every action right that we may express. We know that the ills of personal existence come from mistakes or from abnormal actions. We understand, therefore, that if we could prevent all mistakes we could prevent all ills.

To accomplish this some advocate this system and some that, each one believing that his system is the one that contains the secret. The fact, however, that all systems produce results has led to the belief that results secured through the system of another were secured through the action of evil power* But here the question arises, how can an evil power make correct use of the laws of life; and again, how can evil power know the truth obtained from those laws? For it is a fact that evil in every instance is the opposite, or rather the absence, of truth.

To build a bridge you require mathematics. Without mathematics you cannot build that bridge.

Therefore, whoever can build bridges or who does build bridges, understands mathematical principles. And for anyone to say that such or such a person builds bridges with the aid of an evil power—a power that would naturally tend to eliminate the truth of mathematics as well as remove mathematicians from their positions, is to make a statement too absurd to be considered for a moment among scientific men. Nevertheless, when we come to mental, moral and spiritual fields we make statements every day that are equally absurd; and we even try to prove that such statements are inspiration.

The fact in this connection, however, is simply this, that it is only the good that can produce good results. And it is only through the understanding of certain phases of truth that we can apply the good. We conclude, therefore, that any man, no matter what his beliefs may be, who secures good results in any field understands the truth to that extent..

The whole universe is based upon absolute law. If it were not, space would contain nothing but chaos, and nothing could exist. Therefore everything that is to be done must be done according to law. We cannot go outside of the law if we wish to construct bridges or engines. Neither can we go outside of the law if we wish to build character or make real the ideal. We cannot perform a single good deed without using some of the laws of life. We cannot convey our ideas through language without using some of these laws. We cannot do anything and produce the same results under the same conditions without using one or more of these laws. And to use the laws of life correctly is to use understanding a certain phase of the truth.

Every person is producing certain results in his life. Some of those results are great and others small, but they are results. Therefore everybody knows some of the truth, as it is only through the application of truth that results can be secured. We thus see the folly of claiming any one system to be the only channel through which truth can be found.

The truth is just as universal as life, and in fact is the very essence or soul of life. Therefore everything that lives, lives some of the truth—as much of the truth as present consciousness can comprehend. Every constructive action of the mind opens the way to greater truth. But no mind can act constructively to good advantage as long as a certain interpretation of truth is accepted as final. The fact is that when you accept anything as final you bring your mind to a standstill in that sphere of action. And the fact that the whole world has accepted certain spiritual and metaphysical ideas as final is one reason why real spirituality is found so rarely. The same is true, however, in various fields of mental and intellectual realms. Therefore no matter how remarkable a discovery you may make, if you accept that as final in its own field you stop there; progress is suspended; further growth is retarded along that line.

And after the new discovery has become a system and lost its life, as all truth does when formulated into a system, we are just as much in mental or spiritual darkness as before; for we must bear in mind that every discovery that we look upon as final in its own field loses its soul; that is, it dies, leaving us the shell of mere belief only. This is natural because all belief comes from within. And as soon as we formulate a number of truths into a fixed system, we begin to worship the system, thereby ignoring the life and the spirit of the within. To ignore the within, however, is to turn away from the source of all truth, all life and all power, which means that we separate ourselves from those very things that we wish to secure in greater abundance. In this connection we should also remember that the very moment we look upon a truth as final we cease to rise in search of more. It is only the rising mind that receives the life, the substance and the spirit of things. And it is only that mind that is ever in search of more truth that can really understand truth. We know the truth only while we are steadily moving upward and onward into more truth.

Truth is everywhere, and truth alone does things. Therefore everything that produces results in its own sphere of action demonstrates truth. And whoever has results has truth. Every demonstration is the result of truth, be it in the healing of disease by any method whatever, or the building of a beautiful mansion by any method whatever. Every method that produces results or that emancipates, builds, constructs, beautifies or elevates, is based upon truth and employs truth. This is natural because truth is everywhere, so that every method can touch truth, be fixed or rooted in truth, and be a constant expression of truth.

If every demonstration was not the result of truth some demonstrations would be the result of untruth, which is impossible. The false cannot take away pain at any time. The false cannot invent and construct machinery. The false cannot develop a child into a musical genius. The false cannot write a poem, nor cause barren waste to become a garden of highly developed roses. In brief, the false cannot do anything.

The laws of the body are just as much in the hands of truth as are the laws of the mind or the soul. Therefore a man who builds a house or perfects his physical form, employs the truth just as well as the man who builds character or unfolds cosmic consciousness.

AH life is good. Everything is sacred, and the truth is the foundation of the entire universe. Thus we understand that the only truth is the universal truth;

and the only way to find universal truth is to live in conscious touch with everything that gives expression to life or truth in any form or manner. Universal truth is not encased in this religious system or in that philosophical belief. Universal truth in the spirit of every atom, of every flower, of every creature, of every entity in existence. There is no special path to this truth because every path leads to this truth. It can be found everywhere and in everything. Everything that lives is moving into more and more of this truth, because to live is to move forward, and to move forward is to enter a larger measure of the all truth.

Every mind lives in the truth and actually breathes the very life of truth. Therefore to find more truth we must live more, and not search for truth in any particular system, but to try to enter into closer mental touch with the all truth as it lives and moves in all things.

Your method for finding the truth you may need now; it may be the only method that works for you at present. In like manner the methods that others employ may be the only ones that they can use now. Therefore we must never say that our method is the only method that will work for everybody, or that everybody can find truth now in the same place as we are finding truth now.

In this connection, however, we must watch a certain tendency that is present more or less in all minds. When we find a new method that does the very thing that we have never succeeded in doing before, there is a tendency to exaggerate or overvalue the merit of that method. This tendency intoxicates the mind, so to speak, and magnifies the new discovery, so it appears much larger than it really is. Naturally, we conclude that it is the best of its kind. In fact, must be the best to our view of thinking, because our view at the time is so magnified.

From this belief of the best there is only a tiny step to the belief of the only; and the tendency that produces the former will also produce the latter. Whenever a mind declares that his is the best he is on the way to the belief that his is the only. And if he is not thoroughly balanced he will soon enter the latter view. The reason the mind acts in this way is easily understood when we become familiar with psychological laws. But those who think they have the only way to truth do not study psychological laws, because their belief has limited their minds to the idea that they have found the one only law. However, the very moment that any mind begins to study psychological laws the "only truth" idea will vanish like the darkness before the light.

When we all understand the mind, and also .why we think what we think, all systems of belief will be discarded. Then we will all seek the truth itself directly, and seek it everywhere. The result will be perpetual growth into the truth. We shall then find the truth that gives freedom to the whole life of man—

the truth that develops every part of the being of man for a higher and truer use. Accordingly, the life more abundant will follow. And from such a life comes everything that mind may desire.

5

WHERE WE GET OUR IDEAS.

Ideas do not come to us from the without. The belief that we are living in a world of ready-made ideas upon which we may draw as we like is not true. The human mind is not a mere receptacle into which ideas may flow from some outer source. The ideas that exist in the individual mind are created by that mind, and by that mind alone. The belief that all ideas come from some external source —that we simply have to open our mind to receive them—makes the mind a mere channel through which something may pass from one place to another; or it may make the mind a mere automaton upon which any force from without may act for good or otherwise. This belief, however, is very common, and it is one of the principal obstacles to originality and greatness, as well as to the finding and knowing of real truth.

The belief that man develops by opening more widely his mind so as to receive a greater number of ideas from the cosmic fields about him, tends to prevent the further development of the mind. While the realization of the fact that man develops by creating more and more original ideas of his own will tend to promote further development. Any system of thought or belief, therefore, that compels the mind to accept the ideas of others will retard the progress, not only of the individual but of the race. On the other hand, anything that teaches man how to create his own ideas and do his own original thinking will promote the development of greatness.

It is a well-known fact that every form of greatness comes from original thinking, and those who understand the natures of mind and soul know that original thinking is the direct result of man's power to create consciously his own ideas according to his highest conception of what is truth. The mind that can create ideas has begun to exercise its own creative powers. And when those powers are mastered anything can be created or recreated. Through these powers man can recreate his own personality, his own character and his own mentality. He can recreate his own mental world, change all his exterior surroundings, and create his own destiny.

Man has the power to become a master in the largest sense of that term. And the first step is to create consciously and intelligently his own ideas. To begin, the fact that ideas do not come from without must be realized. We may receive impressions from external sources, but we do not receive ideas from those sources. The only ideas that exist in any mind are the ideas that that mind itself has created.

In this connection we must remember that an idea is not a belief about something, but the result of your own mental conception of that something. You may accept any number of beliefs about things without actually thinking about those things. But when you try to understand those things from your own point of view, you form a mental conception of your own, and the result is ideas of your own. These ideas may be crude, nevertheless, you have begun to exercise your own creative power, and may so develop that power that the future may find you in advance of the greatest minds of the age.

To exercise this creative power try to form mental conceptions of everything that may enter your mind; that is, try to understand all things of which you are conscious by looking at those things from your own individual point of view. Do not ask what others may think about this or that, but ask yourself, What do I think? How do these things appear to me while viewed through the eyes of my own mind? Your conclusion may be imperfect at first, but you are arousing your own creative powers; you are forming mental conceptions in your own mentality; and you are creating ideas of your own. You are therefore developing originality and have entered the path to greatness as well as the path to the higher and better understanding of greater truth.

To bring your mental creative power into full play the more impressions from the without that you admit in your mind the better, provided those impressions have quality and worth; because to form conceptions we must have something about which to think, and both quality and quantity should be sought from every source. Impressions come through the senses, and indicate to consciousness the fact that there is something real back of those phases of life that are represented by the impressions thus received.

When you look at something you gain an impression. But that impression is not at first an idea. The impression simply indicates the existence of something without giving any definite information as to what that something might actually be. If you accept that impression as final on the subject you fail to form any idea of your own with regard to it. Thus your creative power is not brought into action through the coming of that impression, and no original thought is formed. On the other hand, if you proceed to form some definite mental conception about that something, the existence of which was indicated by the impression, you will form an idea of your own, thereby developing the power of original thought.

The same impressions, however, do not originate the same ideas in different minds; nor is this necessary. The purpose is that each individual mind is to form ideas of his own in connection with every impression that is received so that the power of original thought may be developed. To a materialistic mind the sight of a forest may simply suggest lumber and profit; but to a lofty mind the same forest may suggest the beautiful idea of God's first temples; and he may enter to worship in states more sublime than he ever knew before. What ideas we shall form therefore from impressions thus received will depend entirely upon our own attitude and purpose in life. Though if we actually form ideas according to our present capacity we shall take real steps in the right direction.

Our interpretations of things may differ for a time, but if we use these interpretations for the purpose of creating original ideas we shall all reach gradually but surely the same high goal, even though our several paths in the beginning were not the same. We realize therefore the folly of criticizing those who differ from us in their ideas about things, because so long as they are creating ideas of their own they are moving forward, building both mind and character; and accordingly deserve only the highest praise.

We want everybody to become much. We want everybody to live the largest and best life that is possible in their present state of development. And since we know that original thinking is the secret of greater things, we must invariably rejoice whenever we discover an individual who has begun to create his own ideas. The fact that his ideas may! differ from our own should not disturb us, because when a mind begins original thinking that mind will become larger and larger, and will ere long gain just as large an understanding of truth as we have, and possibly much larger still in the course of time.

In dealing with people, therefore, our object should not be to persuade them to accept our system of belief. On the contrary, we should try to encourage them in original thinking. We should try to present methods through which they may become so great in mind and soul that they can understand the whole truth for themselves. The mind that becomes larger and larger will know the truth and live the truth without being persuaded by others. Therefore all our efforts for the race should be directed upon the development of larger minds and greater souls. To promote this purpose original thinking along the lines of seeking, finding and knowing the truth is the one great essential. Let people believe what they like for the present, but do your best, by all means, to stimulate the desire in all minds to create their own individual ideas about everything.

The truth is everywhere. We all can see it if we have sufficient mental capacity; no one has the monopoly; nor is it necessary for us to gain our understanding of truth through certain persons or systems. All minds are equal before the Infinite Mind. And each individual mind must understand the truth through his own mentality. We can know only by using our own power to know. And that power develops through the constant use of creative capacity, that is, original thinking, or the creation of our own ideas about everything about which we may think.

If we wish people to see as much of the true and beautiful as we see, we should help them to develop the same high states of mind. The same mental altitudes produce the same points of view, the same points of view produce the same mental conceptions, and the same mental conceptions produce the same ideas. In consequence, when we reach the heights of great souls we shall see life as they see it; we shall think the same thoughts that they think; and the peace and the joy that they feel we shall feel also.

Do not criticize what you do not understand, or what does not appeal to you. Instead, develop your mind more and more; and what you do not understand today will be simplicity itself tomorrow. We are wasting too much time trying to change each other's belief. If we would all use that time helping each other on to greater heights of understanding and power we should ere long become so highly developed that we all could see all things from all points of view. Then we should all agree in all things without even trying to agree.

We cannot find the truth by following this system or that, but by using the best systems and methods in the development of a superior understanding; and in the use of methods we must remember that impressions or beliefs have no value except as indicators pointing the way to some hidden reality or truth. Therefore those who receive the wisdom of the past, or the impressions of the present, as something to have and to hold, gain absolutely nothing. However, those who try to form original mental conceptions of everything that enters the mind from any source, will not only develop originality and greatness, but will sooner or later form those very ideas that have always produced the greatest things in life.

We are changed, improved or transformed through the renewal of our minds. And this renewal is the result of our creating superior ideas of everything about which we may think. To form superior ideas it is necessary to improve constantly upon all of our mental conceptions; in brief, to accept no conclusion as final, but to try to see all things through a larger and a larger understanding The greatest mistake that can be made in this connection is to accept ideas from other minds without trying to improve upon those ideas in our own minds.

The ideas we think we receive from other minds are not necessarily ideas, but usually only impressions of those ideas, because the only ideas that can exist in any mind are the ones that that mind creates itself. Those impressions, however, that are received from the ideas expressed by others may become instrumental in forming ideas of our own if employed for that purpose; but if they are simply accepted without further thought they are valueless.

Originality comes not by accepting beliefs, but from the creation of superior ideas about all things that are represented by our beliefs. And the more numerous our beliefs or impressions are the better, provided we select only the best. There are some who are trying to develop originality by refusing to listen to other minds, thinking that they must depend wholly upon their own conclusions. But originality does not come by ignoring the thoughts of others. Originality comes by improving upon those thoughts. And since we must know the best thoughts in the world today in order to create something better, we should familiarize ourselves with the best ideas and the best minds everywhere. Then we should try to form superior ideas in our own minds. We may not succeed at once in forming ideas that are superior to those of the master minds, but we will in the effort create ideas of our own, thus taking the path to greatness and the path to greater truth. And by continuing in this path we shall soon rise to those heights from where we can give the world something better than has ever been given before.

To form superior ideas look at the subject under consideration from as many viewpoints as possible and enter into the finest grades of mental life during the process. Learn to feel deeply whenever you think, and try to see the very soul of all thought. All such effort, however, must be gentle, though filled with a strong, penetrating desire that gives the whole attention to the spirit of perfection that permeates all things. Refine the mind by training yourself to think through the feeling of your finest conception of refinement, and hold attention centered upon your highest realization of what may be termed cosmic substance. This substance is the perfect substance from which all substance is formed. Therefore it is the highest and finest that we can think of. It is the least material, and by thinking about it your mind enters into a finer consciousness through which superior ideas will invariably be formed.

Having realized this fine mental life, take up your various beliefs and try to form superior ideas about the principles or realities which those beliefs represent. You will have results almost from the beginning. Then search everywhere for ideas that are superior to your own in order that you can improve upon them all. Whether you do or not you will at any rate improve upon your own power of originality, and to continue in that improvement is to reach those heights in the course of time where you can improve upon almost anything. Through this practice discoveries and inventions of great value may appear to you at any time. In fact, you are liable to do greater things than ever were done before, no matter how insignificant you may be today. By creating your own ideas about all things you begin the development of creative power and there is no limit to what this power can do.

6

THE TWO SIDES OF TRUTH.

Everything in life has two sides. When we view anything from the one side only the result is a half-truth. But when the same thing is viewed from both sides the result will be a whole truth. The physical scientist who ignores metaphysics has therefore nothing but half-truths to present to the world. And the same is true of the metaphysician who ignores the physical side of that which he attempts to study and understand.

A half-truth generally seems plausible, in fact so plausible at times that only a few can detect its incompleteness. But the conclusions of the half-truth invariably mislead the mind at every turn. A half-truth, however, not only misleads the mind, but gradually eliminates the power of discrimination so that the mind finally becomes incapable of finding the truth when real truth does appear. That person that has followed half-truths all his life is unable to know real truth when face to face with it. And as the majority are more or less in this condition this phase of our study of truth becomes extremely important.

Every modern system of belief is filled with half-truths, but it will not be necessary here to analyze them all. A general analysis of the most striking illustrations will be sufficient, as through such an analysis anyone will be able to detect the flaws in the others. One of the most striking of these illustrations in the thinking of half-truths is found in the statement that mind is the only power. At first sight it may appear that the mind is the cause of everything, and that it does everything, but a deeper study reveals the fact that the mind is only one phase of the only power. There is but one power in the universe; that is, one fundamental force of action, but this power differentiates itself into a vast number of phases, and any one phase is as real as any of the others.

We have recently discovered the fact that the mind exercises great power over the body. And for that reason many have come to the conclusion that the mind is the only power that effects the body. But this is a half-truth and comes from viewing the subject from one side only. Many people who accept this view go so far as to say that it is wrong to use anything else but mind whenever we wish to relieve or effect the body. But those who follow half-truths are never consistent; and in consequence, while affirming that mind alone can help the body, they continue to protect the body with physical clothes and feed the body with physical food.

As a rule, people who follow half-truths forget that it is the same power that has created everything, and that therefore the things that are seen are just as real and good as the things that are not seen, and, of course, vice versa. In brief, all things are real in their own sphere of existence, and all things are good in their own proper places.

In this connection we must remember that the mind always acts through agencies; whether these be muscles, nerves, senses, intellect or thought, they are agencies of mind; and one agency is not inferior to another. If it is right for the mind to use thought in removing a physical condition or disease, it is also right for the mind to use muscle in performing a surgical operation, should it be wise and necessary to perform such an operation. In both instances it is the mind acting upon the body through an agency. On the other hand, if it is wrong to perform a surgical operation when some simple remedy would avail, it would also be wrong to waste precious mental energy in overcoming physical ailments that could just as easily be removed by some simple or natural method.

The question is, not what to discard entirely and what to use exclusively; the question is, to determine what means or methods will produce the best and the quickest results now under present conditions. Use any power when that particular power is needed, and use it well, because every power is but an expression of the one Supreme Power. All is good in its place, and all is made for the service of man; therefore all things can be used in adding to the welfare of man.

When you believe that mind is the only power, you limit yourself more and more to such powers as may be expressed on the mental plane. In consequence you will be compelled to depend almost entirely upon mental force, and will be helpless when that force is weakened, which frequently happens with those who neglect the development of everything but mind. So long as you believe that the mind is the only power you open the mental door to mental powers alone. You eliminate all others and cannot come into possession of those marvelous spiritual powers that alone can make man great.

A study of people who believe that mind is the only power, reveals clearly that their work is conducted entirely upon the mental plane; and in too many instances gives expression to the narrowest phases of mentality. When you carry this idea of the allness of mind to its extreme conclusion, you eliminate all the expressions of the mind to that of what may be called mental force or mind vibrations. You will depend upon such actions of mind for everything. You will expect those vibrations to act upon things directly and to do anything desired without the use of agencies. Ability, mental capacity, character, intelligence, talent and, in brief, all the natural functions and powers of the mind will be neglected. All development, therefore, will be retarded, as the whole of attention is centered upon the efforts of mental vibration; that is, the mind acting with a certain purpose in view without the use of agencies through which to act. Finally the mind becomes so dull that it is even incapable of retaining conscious control of its own mental vibrations. In fact, by narrowing itself down to one thing it becomes so small that even that one thing is neither understood nor controlled.

It is therefore evident that by thinking that the mind is the only power, your mind will become so small and so superficial that it will be incapable of original and individual thought. It will be unable to stand upon its own feet and will have to depend wholly upon some fixed system.

Life is complex and gives expression to many powers. Mind is one of these, but only one of many. And if we would develop the power of the mind we must train ourselves to give a larger and a more perfect expression to all the other powers as well. We add to the power and the capacity of every single function by increasing the power of all the other functions. And the leading faculty of any mind will have the greatest ability and capacity when backed up, so to speak, with a number of other faculties that are also strong and highly developed.

Another statement heard frequently among those who see only the one side of truth is this, that everything is all right if we think so. This idea, of course, is founded upon the belief that wrong thought is the only cause of evil or imperfection. But if we should follow this belief to its extreme and inevitable conclusion, we would have to say that thought is everything, and that all else is nothing. If your thinking makes things right or wrong the things themselves can have neither power nor qualities. And if this were true things could not even have existence, because, to exist, a thing must have powers and qualities of some kind.

According to such a belief the cheapest clothing would be rich and rare if we only thought so; the most homely face would be charmingly beautiful if we only thought so; the most ordinary music would be simply inspiring if we thought so; and the worst meal that was ever prepared would be perfectly delicious if we thought it was. Thousands of other conclusions equally absurd would naturally follow our attempt to describe things according to this belief. But this is always the case with half-truths. They seem plausible as long as they are not closely examined.

If we should adopt the belief that everything is all right if we think it is, we would soon be unable to distinguish between degrees of perfection; our judgment would become so poor that we could see no difference between the common and the worthy, between the homely and the beautiful, between the false and the true. To us everything would be lovely, but loveliness would mean nothing more to us than the most superficial sentiment. We would say that all things are good because we think so, but we should be unable to understand what goodness actually means, therefore would fail to grow in the realization of goodness.

The whole truth in this connection is that when things are wrong your thinking they are right will not make them right. But you can through the proper use of your thought cause things to change and become right. The way you think, when in the presence of wrong things, will determine to a very great extent how you are to be affected by those things, and also how much those things may be changed by your action under the circumstances. But the things themselves, as well as their present conditions, are just as real as your thought, though they will obey the power of your thought completely if that power is properly employed.

You may listen to the most beautiful music, but you will fail to enjoy it if you are in a critical frame of mind. The lack of enjoyment will in this instance come not from things, but from your perverted thought about things. Your wrong thought, however, had no effect whatever upon the music. The music was good in spite of what you thought, but your own thought prevented you from getting any good out of the music. On the other hand, you may listen to music that is full of discord, but if you refuse to be disturbed by discord you will remain in harmony. The fact, however, that you remain in harmony will not make the music harmonious, proving conclusively that under such circumstances your state of mind affects only yourself, and does not effect those things that exist outside of yourself.

However, you may try to think that inharmonious music is actually sweet and lovely, and may wholly succeed through this suggestion in rendering yourself unconscious to the discord. You may in consequence enjoy the music to some extent, but your judgment of music will suffer. Should you practice this method frequently the best music would after a while fail to give more enjoyment than ordinary music, and you could not possibly enter into the realization of the soul of music itself.

If you undertake a certain work and think you are going to fail, the confusion of mind and the scattering of forces produced by such a frame of mind, will almost invariably produce failures. On the other hand, if you think you are going to succeed you will concentrate all your forces on success; accordingly, those forces will work together for success and will place success within reach, though of course work and ability must be added before results can be secured. The fact that you think you are going to succeed will not alone produce success, but to think that you are going to succeed is one of the essentials. In fact, it is quite indispensable.

A number of ambitious people at the present time who have no ability, and who do not care to develop themselves, believe that everything will come to them if they simply think success. Success, however, does not come in this way. If you wish to succeed you must have ability and you must apply it thoroughly as well as wisely. You must have confidence in yourself and faith in abundance. You must press on with all the determination that is within you, working constantly in the right states of mind, and turn all the forces of thought, talent and ability upon the goal in view.

The way we think affects to an extraordinary degree everything we do and everything with which we come in contact. But mere thinking is not all that is required to make things right, nor will things turn from bad to good simply because we think they are good. There are methods through which all things can be changed, but such methods will not be employed simply by our saying or thinking that things are what they are not. If we try to make ourselves believe that things are what they are not, we not only delude ourselves, but we carry on a sort of mesmeric process that will sooner or later make invalids of our minds, and so weaken all our faculties or talents that we will soon be incapable of achieving anything worthwhile.

The real student of life takes things as he finds them, regardless of what they may be. If things are not right he admits it, and goes to work doing something to make them right. On the other hand, if they are good he is fully able to enjoy them to the fullest extent because his appreciation is not clouded by self-delusions. The strong soul is never disturbed or made unhappy when meeting things out of place. He does not have to suggest to himself that all is well, when it is not, in order to keep himself composed. He knows that he is ready for any emergency, that he is equal to any occasion, that he has the power to overcome any adversity, and that he has the ability to make all things right. He is therefore composed in the presence of wrong and fully ready to do something definite to make the wrong right. Such a mind can see the whole truth about the subject of right and wrong. The undeveloped side or the exterior side, with its possibilities, is recognized and understood. And that power within that can develop these possibilities is recognized and applied. Thus the imperfect is changed into some degree of perfection, and evil is transformed into actual good.

The mind that meets life in this way will constantly make things better and will develop superiority in himself through that mode of thinking alone. On the other hand, the person who thinks that everything is lovely will leave things the way they are, improving nothing, not even himself; thus he will continue to remain in the same small self-deluded state. He may have health, peace and happiness in a measure in his little world, but how small that little world will be. And nothing in the world at large will be better off because he has lived.

In this connection we must remember that it is of the first importance to recognize and learn to apply the immense power of thought, but that power is not applied simply by thinking that things are as we wish them to be. The power of thought works through methods; that is, through the living of what we think, and through the doing of those things that make for growth, quality and worth.

Another half-truth that has deceived thousands of well-meaning minds is expressed in the statement, "If you see evil in others it is because you are evil yourself." There is, however, some truth back of this idea though this truth would be better expressed if we should say, 'There is a tendency of the human mind to believe that others have the same weaknesses that we have." Though here we must remember that this is only a tendency and is by no means the rule in every mind. We know that if a man is selfish he finds it difficult to think of Others as unselfish; but the cause in his case is simply a narrow viewpoint.

So long as we live in a certain mental attitude we are inclined to look at all things through the colored glasses of that attitude; in consequence our judgment is biased. However, when the judgment is unbiased and the mind can see all things from all points of view, all things will be seen as they are. Such a mind can see the wrong in others without being wrong himself, because he can see all things from all points of view. The higher we ascend in the scale the more clearly we can see the mistakes of the world and the less mistakes we ourselves will make. But we not only see the mistakes, we also see the cause and the remedy; and we do not condemn.

Though we see all wrong we can forgive all wrong because we can see the cause of it all, remembering the great truth, "To know all is to forgive all." Thousands of well-meaning idealists condemn themselves for seeing evil in others, believing that they are in bondage to the same wrongs, but this is simply a delusion coming from viewing only one side of the truth in the matter. When you can see everything, you can see the imperfect as well as the perfect, both in others and in yourself. It is not wrong to see the mistakes of others, but it is wrong to condemn. For it is certainly a fact that when we condemn wrong we perpetuate wrong, and also tend to produce that same wrong in ourselves.

When you actually believe that you have a certain failing you tend to create that failing through your own thinking. The mind has the power to create any sort of condition in the system and employs all deep seated beliefs, ideas or impressions as models. Therefore, by believing that you are a sinner you make sin the pattern for your thinking, and all your thoughts will be created more or less in the likeness of sin. When we understand this law we understand what a horrible mistake it is to think of ourselves as sinners; and we also discover why the majority continue to remain weaklings from the cradle to the grave.

If you wish to eliminate sin, evil and worry from your life study metaphysics and psychology. Learn to give the creative powers of your life more ideal patterns. Learn to create your thoughts after the likeness of purity, truth, goodness, strength, wholeness and virtue. You will gradually become more and more like those thoughts because, "As a man thinketh in his heart so is he."

The belief that we have the same sins or evils that we see in others is a belief that is self-contradictory at every point. For if we see evil in others simply because that same evil is in ourselves it is the evil in ourselves that we see. If that evil was not in ourselves we would not see it in others: but if it is only in ourselves it does not exist at all in the others. And if this be true, why do others see sin in us? They must according to the theory be just the same kind of sinners as we are. The fact that they see wrong in us proves that the same wrong exists in them, while according to our belief the wrong does not exist in them, but exists only in ourselves. We must admit, therefore, that the wrong we see is not simply in ourselves, but also in others, otherwise the belief would not hold good all around. Nevertheless, if we admit this we contradict the very idea upon which the belief is based, proving that the whole thing is but an illusion. We may imagine that others have certain wrongs that they have not, but the fact that we imagine these wrongs existing in others does not prove that these wrongs exist at all, either in others or in ourselves. For, suppose we see in others what is not there; suppose we imagine others having certain failings because we have them; suppose some of us at times do this; does that prove that the pure mind is unable to see what is not pure? It does not. It simply proves that when the imagination is not under control we may imagine many things that do not have existence anywhere.

When your eyes are open you will see everything that is to be seen, be it black or white. And the mind that is pure certainly has the same power to see with open eyes, that the mind has that is not pure. In fact it is only the pure mind that sees all that is good and all that is evil. The impure mind is partially blinded. However, when we realize that evil in itself is not bad, but simply an undeveloped state, we conclude that it is no more of an evil to see evil than it is to see a green apple.

The green apple is undeveloped. It is not ready to be eaten, but it is not on that account bad of itself, though it would produce undesirable effects if it were eaten in its present condition. The same is true of all other things that are undeveloped. We think they are evil because we have found it painful to use them in their undeveloped state. We have not realized that the pain came, not because the fruit was bad, but because we tried to eat it before it was ripe.

7

STRIKING ILLUSTRATIONS OF HALF TRUTHS.

Everyday experience has demonstrated the fact again and again that when we look for trouble we usually find it. And also that when we look for health, peace, harmony and abundance we almost invariably gain possession of those things in a greater or a lesser measure. This fact has led a number to believe that we meet only what we look for. But this conclusion is nothing but a half truth. We know that we meet a number of things in daily life that we never looked for, and many things that we even never thought of. Almost daily we come in contact with conditions that do not belong to us and that have no legitimate place in our world. Therefore to say that we .meet only what we look for is not to speak the truth.

Besides, when we live in the belief that we meet only what we look for, we condemn ourselves for many times as many wrongs as we are responsible for. And to condemn ourselves for any wrong is to impress that wrong upon the subconscious. What is impressed upon the subconscious will bear fruit after its kind; therefore when you condemn yourself for any wrong you sow a seed in your mind that will later on produce more wrongs of the same kind. This is a fact of extraordinary importance and clearly explains why it seems so difficult for most people who want to be right to live up to the doctrines they profess. If we wish to emancipate ourselves from sickness, trouble and discord, want and misfortune we must not sow any more seeds of that sort. And to condemn ourselves for any wrong is to sow seeds that will produce another harvest of those wrongs.

We are living in a world where many things are imperfect. Things in general are in a state of becoming and many parts are incomplete, but those things are not incomplete because we may be looking for incompleteness. They are incomplete because the world is not finished. And so long as the world remains unfinished those things will remain incomplete whether we look for incompleteness or not. So long as we are moving about in the world we will meet the imperfect whether we are looking for it or not, but those imperfections will not do us any harm if we meet them in the proper attitude. Green apples will not give you pain so long as they are not taken into the system. Nor will incomplete circumstances and conditions disturb you if you do not take those conditions into your mind. The fact is what things are to do to us will depend largely upon what we in the first place proceed to do with things.

When you go on a journey and find an immense rock in the way you do not ask yourself what wrong you have done in the past that you should meet this obstacle. The rock came there through causes that are entirely distinct from the causes of your individual existence, and you found that rock because you went that way. But why did you go that way? The answer can be found, though this will lead us into hair-splitting arguments regarding the nature of motives. However, so long as you have errands here and there and everywhere you will find obstacles in the way due to the fact that the world is not finished. But instead of becoming discouraged about those obstacles you should learn to surmount them.

In this connection we may well ask, that if we never looked for obstacles and never expected to meet them, could we not go about our work without meeting obstacles at all? For is it not true that there is a smooth path to every place, and that he who seeks such a path will always find it? It is true that there is a smooth path to every place in the domains of life, or rather the possibilities of such a path, but this path is not ready-made. Each individual must make it for himself to fit his own requirements.

The whole truth in this connection is that we have the power to make every path smooth as we go on. We can remove all obstacles and change all misfortunes, sorrows and adversities into such things as may be more desirable or more advantageous. The average person is constantly looking for smooth paths that are all ready; that is, paths that are made smooth by someone else, but such paths do not exist. You cannot use the path of another and at the same time fulfill the purpose of your own life. And though such a path may be smooth to him, it might prove the most difficult way that you could possibly undertake.

The reason why so many fail to realize their ideals is, because they are looking for ready-made advantages, expecting to find them because they are constantly looking for them. But here we must remember that the only things we can use to advantage are the things we ourselves create at such times as we have greater things in mind. It is true, however, that what we are constantly looking for we tend to create in our own minds. And as like attracts life, what we create within ourselves we shall naturally attract in our external circumstances.

When you are constantly looking for trouble you will be thinking trouble— thus your mind will be troubled and confused. You will be constantly making mistakes, and mistakes always lead to real troubles in the external world. It is therefore simple to understand why the person who is looking for trouble usually meets trouble. But we all meet troubles that we never look for, that we never thought of, that we never created; which fact proves that it is not true that we meet only what we look for.

If we wish to be free from trouble, we should never look for trouble, never think about trouble, never expect trouble and never create trouble. And in addition when we meet such troubles as others have produced we should refuse to become troubled. You do not have to eat green apples. Neither do you have to take into your mind troubles that others have produced. Be in peace, be in poise, be in harmony, be strong, be your own master and resolve to think only peace, regardless of what your surrounding conditions may be. And this anyone can do just as easily as he can move the muscles of his hands or feet.

When you meet troubles or misfortunes do not condemn yourself, whether you are to blame or not. Troubles and misfortunes come from mistakes, and the more you condemn yourself the more mistakes you will make. When in the midst of wrong forgive yourself and forgive everybody; let the wrong go; drop it completely from your mind; rise out of it and resolve to recreate everything for the better. You will soon be free. And you will also turn all misdirected energies to good account for the fact is all things in your life will work together for good / when you desire the good, and the good only.

Every time you forgive yourself you decrease your tendency to do wrong. And if the forgiveness of yourself is followed by a positive ascension of mind into the higher and the better, the tendency to do wrong will be removed, and a strong tendency to do the right will appear instead. When all the tendencies of life have a tendency to do right and build the greater you will naturally do the right. You will be good not because you try to be good, but because it has become your nature to be good. And this is the goal we all have in view.

When you forgive yourself for everything and try to surmount everything you steadily develop that power that can surmount, transform and overcome everything. And ere long the meeting of trouble will not be a misfortune to you because you can change it instantaneously to something good. Although we shall meet many things that we never looked for, and encounter many wrongs for which we are not responsible, still we are equal to every occasion if we continue to be our best. And what is more, *the things we meet in life constitute the raw material from which we may build a larger life and a greater destiny. Whatever you meet, be it pleasing or otherwise, remember it is raw material. You can take that material and turn it to excellent use in the creating of a stronger personality, a more brilliant mind and a more beautiful soul.*

Man is an alchemist in his own domain. He can change the basest metals of his life into the finest gold. He can transform every element within his' own existence and make it what he may wish it to be. And though it is true that we shall meet many things that we do not look for, many adversities that we did not create, still we should count it all joy because we can make good use of everything and turn all things to good account.

The fact that each individual has the power to recreate his own world has led many to believe that the individual is the creator of everything that appears in his world. And therefore it has frequently been stated as a law that we find in life exactly what we put into it. This, however, is another half-truth, because no person lives to himself, for himself or by himself. Each individual finds in his life many things that others have placed there both before and after birth, though each individual is at liberty to use all these things according to his own aims and desires.

Every individual act will affect thousands of lives for good or otherwise, depending upon the nature of the act. Therefore, every individual must learn not only how to place the best in all those lives that he may affect, including his own, but also how to use those things that constantly flow into his life from other sources. In this connection we meet a most important fact, for it is evident that the person who believes that we find in life only what we put into it will naturally turn his whole attention to the art of placing the best in his own life, but will not give any attention to the art of using to advantage what comes from others. It is therefore evident that such a person will soon find himself in a sea of problems that he cannot solve—problems that have arisen through his coming in contact with the hundreds of things that naturally flow into his life from the lives of others.

To give your best to life you must make the very best use of everything that you possess; but in the using of things, you constantly come in touch with the world in general, and you will have to know how to dispose of those things, be they good or otherwise, that invariably come into your life through this contact. However, if you are unable to overcome the adversities that you meet in the world, and do not know how to make practical use of the good things you find you will be at the mercy of your circumstances. You will gain little or nothing from the opportunities that may surround you because you have not learned the art of taking advantage of opportunities; and as you do not know how to remove obstacles you will be practically helpless. In such a condition you can do nothing, neither with the possibilities that exist within you nor with those that exist all about you. You can give nothing of value to life. You will sow nothing in your own world and you will reap nothing in your own world. And what conies from others you cannot use because you do not know how.

The whole truth on this great subject is this: We find in life what we put into life and what we take out of life. What we put into life is the result of our own individual talents, powers and possessions. And what we take out of life is the result of our individual use of that which comes from other sources; that is, from persons, things, circumstances and events. Others may place sorrow in your life, but it will not be sorrow to you if you understand how to make all things work together for greater good. The world may place rare opportunities in your very path. In fact, the world is constantly placing such opportunities in the path of everybody, but unless you know how to take advantage of those opportunities they will be of no value to you. It is the same with all other things that may come to us from other sources. If they are good their value will depend upon how well we use them. If they are not good they will not affect us adversely unless we permit them to do so.

Every day we find things in life that we never put into life; some good, some not. The good things we often pass by not knowing their value, while those things that are not good disturb us because we do not know how to turn misdirected energies to good account. The universe is a rich gift to man. Each individual is heir to all that the race has done, not because he has put an equal amount into the life of the race, but because he is a member of the race, and a necessary part. Each part is necessary to the whole. Therefore each individual has the privilege to take into his own life everything that he can use. And he can do this without depriving anybody of anything because there is more than enough to go around. However, nothing is of value to you unless you can turn it to practical use. And what is important, you cannot turn your life to practical use unless you can also turn to practical use those things that come to you through the lives of others. And as others are constantly giving you things that are good and things that are not good you must understand what to do with all such gifts. If we do not use things we will be used by things. And if we do not learn the art of using what comes from others we shall be so completely controlled by circumstances that we shall be unable to apply our own personal talents. This will prevent us from putting anything into life, and also from taking anything out of life. Life to us therefore, under such circumstances, will be practically empty. Though we have it in our power to change those circumstances and gain a life of richness and high worth instead.

8

THE SUBCONSCIOUS FACTOR.

Extensive investigations along metaphysical and psychological lines have demonstrated conclusively that thought exercises an extraordinary power in the life of man. And since this power is found to act, not only in every part of the mind, but in every atom of the body as well, many have come to believe that everything in man, good or otherwise, comes from thought, and that man is as he thinks, and only as he thinks. Strictly speaking, it is the truth that man is as he thinks; but that abstract thought is the only cause of his thinking is not the whole truth. A large number of metaphysicians and idealists, however, have taken this idea as the whole truth, and have in consequence, not only been misled in every pursuit of the truth, but have failed to apply the power of thought in such a way as to accomplish what really can be accomplished through systematic and scientific thinking.

The power of thought, however, is very great, as it is the powers of mind and thought that determine what every part of the body is to do. It is conscious thought that causes the voluntary motions of the body, and subconscious thought that causes the involuntary. Before you can move a muscle you must exercise the power of the conscious mind, and before your food can be digested the subconscious mind must give action to the functions of digestion. It is the subconscious mind that controls the circulation, digestion, assimilation, the process of physical reconstruction, all functional activities, and all those actions in the body or the mind that are not originated by the will. The subconscious also controls habits and characteristics, mental tendencies, the actions of character and the scope, capacity and present power of all the faculties and talents. But the subconscious mind does its work automatically and acts according to directions received from the conscious mind. It is therefore possible for the conscious mind to change gradually the actions of the subconscious, or to bring the subconscious back to normal action when it is not performing its functions properly. This fact proves that man is absolute master of his entire personality. Though he must follow the laws of life to exercise that mastership.

When the conscious mind worries, the subconscious mind is thrown out of harmony and therefore fails to perform its functions properly. That part of the subconscious that controls the functions of digestion will be misdirected and indigestion will follow. That part that controls the reconstruction of the body will through perverse action create abnormally looking cells, and the body will begin to look old and ugly. Other functions are similarly affected, not only by worry, but by every other action of the conscious mind.

The subconscious also effects the chemical actions, vital actions, nerve actions and all the various forces of the personality. Though the subconscious never modifies its regular actions until impressed to do so by the conscious mind. We may therefore state it as a general law that the personal man is what the subconscious mind causes him to be. But the subconscious mind does only what the conscious mind directs it to do. And since the conscious mind is controlled by the understanding and the will each individual can determine what he wants the subconscious mind to do, thus proving the mastership of man.

The statement, "As a man thinketh in his heart so is he," might be transposed to read, the personal man is the result of what the subconscious mind is, thinks and does; because it is the subconscious that constitutes the heart of mentality or the vital center of the entire mental world. Since the personal man is what the subconscious mind causes him to be, and since the subconscious does only what it is directed to do by the conscious mind, the great question before us is, how to use the conscious mind in such a way that the subconscious will always be directed to do what we want to have done

However, before we proceed further, we must remember that after the subconscious has begun to do a certain thing it will continue to do that particular thing until the conscious mind directs otherwise. After you have made the subconscious perform a certain function it will continue to perform that function not only in yourself but in your children and children's children for generations and generations, or until it is stopped by the actions of the conscious mind in any individual. What is impressed upon the subconscious in one generation will be inherited by the next. Though each individual can remove undesirable hereditary conditions by changing the action of his own subconscious mind.

Through gradual development ages ago, the subconscious mind was trained to make the digestive organs digest when anything entered the system. It was trained to cause the eyes to wink every few seconds so as to keep the eyeball moist. It was trained to cause the saliva to flow whenever anything of an edible nature entered the mouth. It was trained to cause the gastric juice to flow when the food entered the stomach. It was trained to manufacture a certain amount of these juices m the system every day. It was trained to remove the old cells in every part of the body every few months and cause new cells to be formed in their places. In brief, it was trained to cause everything to be done in the body that is being done in the body, and it will continue to do those things of itself. The subconscious will not have to be directed anew to do those things. It was properly directed a long time ago through the gradual needs of man. It does not require a second command. But it can be directed to do those things better. And it can be trained to do special things both in mind and body that have never been done before.

The subconscious can be trained to do almost anything. Therefore there is practically no limit to the possibilities that are latent in the human system. In the average person, however, the subconscious fails to control the physical functions as perfectly as it might. And it does not in any person bring the system up to the most perfect state of being and action. The reason is it has not been directed along those more perfect lines.

The conscious mind in the average person permits the subconscious to be the way it is or the way it has been from one generation to another. The average man therefore is the way the race has been thinking because he thinks the same way. His life and his actions are the result of the sum total of the habits that have been inherited in generations past. He can, however, improve upon these habits, tendencies or inherited conditions through the training of the subconscious mind to do its work better than that work has been done in the past. That this is possible we know through the fact that experimental psychology has proven the susceptibility of the subconscious to do whatever the conscious mind may direct.

In the average person the subconscious has been trained to create an older and weaker body every year, but it can just as easily be trained to create a stronger body and a more vigorous body every year. The subconscious has also been trained to keep the body in a limited state, and to cause those faculties actually to lose their power and brilliancy after a certain period of life has been reached. But the subconscious, if properly trained, can just as easily cause all the faculties to become stronger and more brilliant every year no matter how long a person may live. The subconscious can also be trained to do things in mind or body that no one has done before. We realize, therefore, that the individual man not only is in the present what he thinks in the present; that is, the sum total of his thought habits, but also that he may become in the future whatever he may train his subconscious mind to think and express. The problem, however, is to train the subconscious properly, or in other words to make the thought of the heart what we wish it to be.

And it is in our attempt to regulate the thought of the heart, which means the same as the thought of the subconscious, that a number of half-truths have arisen in modern systems of belief. In the first place, we have believed that it was thought in general that moulds the personality of man. And we have tried to change our thought on the surface without any regard to the fact that no thought

50

can affect the system until it becomes subconscious. In the second place we have tried to change thought by acting directly upon our own minds without taking into consideration the environments in which we might be placed at the time. In the third place we have tried to master mind and thought by simply using will force, paying no attention to the law through which the will must act in order to demonstrate and exercise this larger self-control.

Concerning the first mistake nothing further need be stated. The preceding pages have made the fact clear that the thought of the heart is synonymous with the mental actions of the subconscious mind, and that no change can be brought about in the mind or the body until the desired change in the actions of the subconscious has been produced. And in this connection it is well to state that every thought, desire or action of the conscious mind will, if deeply felt, become subconscious.

Another fact of equal importance is that the personal man is not the result simply of what he thinks, but of that thought that is placed in action. And by action in this connection we mean all action in the human system, whether that action be mental, chemical, vital, functional or muscular. Also that no thought, desire or will can produce action at any time unless it is made subconscious. We realize that every thought that is to affect the system must be created with the tendency to produce action, and must be deeply impressed upon the subconscious mind.

To produce a change in any part of mind or body the conscious mind must first, create that thought that has the power to produce the necessary change. Second, the conscious mind must will to apply that thought in actual tangible action. And third, that thought must be impressed upon the subconscious, or rather, the subconscious must be directed to carry that thought into positive action.' Why the majority of idealists have so frequently failed to demonstrate long sought for changes in their minds or personalities after they have fully changed their mode of thinking is therefore evident. They have followed a half truth and have done their work largely for nought. In other words, they have not removed inherited subconscious beliefs and established actual truth in their places.

A group of half-truths that is very detrimental has come from the belief that we can change our thought by simply willing to change our minds; and also that we can change our thought without changing our thinking. But here we must remember that thought, and thought forces, as well as mental images and ideas, invariably come from thinking. Therefore we must change our thinking before we can change our habits of thought or our subconscious thought.

To think, is to actually exercise the mind in forming definite conceptions about something; that is, to try to understand that about which we may be thinking. To change our thinking it is therefore necessary to change our conceptions of those things with which we may come in daily contact. That is, we must not only change our ideas about ourselves and about certain abstract principles, but we must change our minds about everything in our environment. We must try to gain a higher viewpoint in our relation to all things, thereby gaining a better conception and a truer understanding of all things. In brief, we must remove the imperfect beliefs of the subconscious, because it is the beliefs of the subconscious, that cause man to be what he is, and establish a higher understanding of truth along all lines in the place of those beliefs.

Many metaphysicians and students of idealism define environment as a mere reflection of the mind of the individual. Therefore, according to their philosophy, environment will change immediately the individual himself changes. But that this is a half-truth is easily proven; and it is a belief that has been most misleading. To change himself man must change his thought. To change his thought he must change his thinking. And to change his thinking he must change his conception of everything with which he may come in contact. But if he thinks that his environment is simply a reflection of his own thought, his conception of his environment will constitute zero in his mental world. In fact, that conception will involve nothing, and a mental conception that has nothing in it is simply a state of ignorance.

He therefore knows nothing definite about the nature of his environment, and the man who does not understand his environment will naturally accept the conclusions of his senses, which are always more or less imperfect. Accordingly, his thought concerning his environment will be wrong thought, or at any rate incomplete. And it is not possible to improve something that we do not clearly understand. If a man's environment is the reflection of his own mind then environment does not exist as a separate thing. According to such philosophy it becomes impossible to think of environment because you can form mental conceptions only of those things that have individual existence. This proves conclusively that the man who thinks of his environment as a mere reflection of his own mind cannot possibly know anything about his environment. And we may repeat that we cannot improve upon that which we do not clearly understand.

However, whatever we may see, or hear or believe will impress the mind. Such impressions will cause the mind to form conceptions about those external things from which the impressions come. From these conceptions will come ideas and thoughts, many of which will affect the personality in one or more places. Therefore the man who does not try to understand the real nature of those things that exist about him will absorb indiscriminately such views as are suggested by the senses. In consequence he will make no intelligent selection of his ideas, and his thinking will be controlled largely by such ideas as are suggested by his environment.

And no man can control himself or improve himself whose thinking is controlled by environment. But to say that the visible universe is unreal, or that tangible things are mere illusions, and that material substance has no existence, is to bring about the same effect. The man that has such views will be controlled both by environment and by such persons as he may accept as authority.

To change your own life and think what you want to think you must form a definite mental conception about everything with which you may come in contact. And this conception must be as high as your mind can possibly reach. In fact, it must be composed of a higher and finer understanding of actual truth. You are as you think in the subconscious; therefore to change yourself you must change your subconscious thought. However, you change your thought not by willing to change your mind, but by changing your mind about all things. You make the proper use of the will, not when you try to force the mind to change, but when you try to direct the mind toward higher and higher points of view.

When you begin to look at all things from the higher point of view all your thoughts will change of themselves. Then if you give this change of thought action in practical life, and direct the subconscious to act with those new ideas you will cause your entire personality to change to correspond. And every such change will be a decided improvement, because you have eliminated in a measure the imperfect or lesser beliefs of the subconscious, and placed in their stead a larger measure of actual truth.

9

THE REAL AND THE UNREAL.

All systems of thought have searched for the causes of good and evil, and several phases of thought have developed the belief that "It is all in yourself." But to reduce this belief to its last analysis is to come to the conclusion that there is no power in the universe outside of the mind of the individual, and therefore nothing has existence except the mind of man. The fact is, however, that every force and element in the universe does have a power of its own, but what that power has to do with the individual will depend directly upon how he relates himself to that power.

Man does not possess the only power, but he does possess the power to determine how all other powers are to be used. Therefore, final results will depend upon him. What is to be in his own world lies entirely with him. But he cannot use properly those powers that exist about him so long as he believes that those powers have no existence. We cannot study and understand that which we believe to be unreal.

To illustrate a leading phase of this idea we will say that you dislike decayed apples, which is natural. But the cause of that dislike is not wholly in your own taste. The cause lies partially in the nature of the apple, which is no longer wholesome. You can prevent the disagreeable sensation of such a food, however, if you avoid it. But to continue to eat that apple, believing that the dislike is all in yourself, will not remove the disagreeable sensation. It may seem to be absent for a while, but that seeming absence will be due to the deadening of your sense of taste caused by strong suggestion. The deadening effect of suggestion, however, is neither permanent nor desirable, therefore in the course of time you will have to reap all the consequences that naturally follow the practice of eating such apples.

The same illustration will hold good with respect to every element and force in existence. You cannot control or determine the effect of things upon yourself by trying to think that they have no existence, but rather by learning how to use those things. True, it is possible to imagine that certain things are disagreeable when they are not, but that is hysteria, which, of course, is all in yourself.

Hysteria, however, is an abnormal condition and we cannot understand the normal through the study of experiences that come from the abnormal.

The proper course to pursue is not to deny the existence of things, but to try to understand more perfectly the real existence of things. Through this understanding we shall learn how to use things. And when we can use things properly we have it in our power to produce what results we may desire.

The idea that all is good is, from a certain point of view, exact truth, but as usually interpreted it is not the whole truth. To state that all that is real is good would be the whole truth. But to state that all temporal conditions as well are good would not be the truth. A disagreeable condition is not good, but the original power producing that condition is good and produces evil only when misdirected. Many idealists when meeting wrongs or adversity declare indifferently that all is good, and in consequence make no efforts to produce a change. They may in this way avoid evil consequences for a short time, but they do so by mentally running away, so to speak, from trouble. The troubles, however, that we try to run away from always follow sooner or later, and never fail to come upon us again in the course of time.

The habit of saying that all is good, no matter what may happen, will invariably lead to extreme mental blindness, and the judgment will become so obtuse that nothing is seen or understood any more as it really is. This habit therefore must be strictly avoided by all whose object is to find the whole truth.

The whole truth in this connection is, that everything is produced by a power that is good in itself. It is possible, however, to misdirect anything that may proceed from that power, and a lack of knowledge on the part of man may cause these misdirections ; therefore it is the understanding in man that alone can prevent them or correct them after they have been made.

To gain this understanding the mind should establish itself in the consciousness of that state of being where the good is realized as absolute good; and from that attitude deal with the conviction that the power back of things is good, and also that things can be changed to become exactly like that power. In other words, the mind should act from the viewpoint of the consciousness of the real which is always good, and thereby gradually eliminate those adverse condition? that manifest as evil or unrealities.

The discovery that the source of everything that is expressed through the personality exists potentially in the within has led many to believe that if the within were developed the without would take care of itself. But we must remember that the objective mind must be highly cultivated before the superior qualities of the subjective mind can find complete expression. To illustrate, a good musician needs a good instrument. Though all things come from the within it is necessary to apply those things upon the without in such a way that the superior qualities of the interior life produce the same superiority in the external life.

Here we must remember that there is a vast difference between being conscious of the ideal and making that ideal real. In like manner there is a difference between dreaming and acting, between visions and tangible results. The visions are necessary, but they must be carried out. They will not of themselves become tangible realities. And that is something that can be brought about only through the efforts of the objective mind. To impress the subconscious with a certain idea is to cause a corresponding expression to come forth, but that expression must be taken up and used. The subconscious expression brings out the material, but the objective mind must go to work and use that material if results are to be gained.

Many idealists believe that they can think anything, do anything, eat anything or live in any way they like because all is good; therefore nothing can do them any harm. And the idea would be true if we were living absolutely in the real, or what may be termed the ultimate. But the human race has not as yet reached that stage. We are gradually approaching the absolutely real wherein there is absolute good; but we have not entered that state, therefore we must deal with things as they are in our present state of development.

When you believe that you can do anything at any time you will violate natural law at almost every turn. But laws were not made to be violated. They are made to lead us into the new, the higher and the better; therefore they must be followed in every form and manner if we have greater things in view. Whenever you violate law there will be harm, injury and suffering whether you think that all is good or not. But when you live so completely in the understanding of the real and the true that you discern the purpose of all law you will never violate any law. You will have no desire to do as you please. Your whole desire will be to conform with the law of your life because you know that every phase of that law is a path to greater things.

At the present time you frequently hear the statement, "I am able to do anything because I am one with the Infinite." But this is not the truth if applied to the present moment. We cannot do anything at the present moment even though it is true that we are one with the Supreme, because there are only certain things for which this present state of existence is adapted. And to try to go outside of that adaptation would be to violate the law of life. We can do today only what we are ready for today, and no more. The majority, however, do not do what they are ready for. There are only a few that are always at their best.

No one can be his best unless he is in harmony with the Infinite and works in conscious unity with Supreme Power. And he who is his best in this sense can do anything that may be necessary to make the present moment complete. But he cannot do in the present that which belongs to some future moment. There are too many, however, who are living almost exclusively for the future, doing very little to make the present complete. For that reason they are never their best in the present, and fail to promote a natural and orderly advancement of existence.

In this connection it is highly important to understand that when we make the sweeping statement that we can do anything now, we tend to scatter thought and consciousness over such a wide area of future possibilities that the present moment will receive but a fraction of the power that we have the ability to apply now. It is a great truth, however, that he who lives and thinks and works in harmony with the Supreme can do everything now that is necessary to make the present moment full and complete.

Another mistaken idea that has arisen among minds who do not fully understand the relation of the real to the unreal, is that the experiences of the senses are illusions. From certain points of view, however, this idea seems plausible. But the plausible is not always true. To state that the senses always mislead, is to admit that we can know nothing and convey nothing, because we have used our senses in every effort that is made to learn facts or convey facts to others. In brief, we have used our senses to learn that the senses do not exist, or that the experiences of the senses are illusions. But if all the experiences of the senses are illusions, then even this extraordinary knowledge would also be an illusion. To make the statement therefore that all experiences or that most of the experiences of the senses are illusions, is to contradict the statement itself absolutely.

The person who depends upon the senses to receive information and who depends upon the senses of others to have that information conveyed, must not state that the senses always mislead, for according to that very theory the information he is trying to convey will be nothing but a bundle of misleading statements. You may think that you have found the result of pure reason, that reason that knows without using the senses, but to convey your discovery to others they must employ their senses, and if the senses always mislead it would be impossible for you to teach pure reason to others.

If the senses are not reliable no one can teach anybody anything. And if this were true we would all be in perpetual darkness and could neither give nor receive information of any kind. Our effort, therefore, to lead each other out of the beliefs of sense experience would involve nothing but mental chaos. But the fact that we can talk coherently about the senses proves that senses are not always unreliable. In the world of illusion the same causes never produce the same effects, but in the world of sense the same causes under the same conditions invariably produce the same effects; which fact proves that it is not the senses that are unreliable, but that our use of the senses sometimes is imperfect. The whole truth is that the senses convey wrong information only when reason accepts certain conclusions as final before all the viewpoints have been taken.

To state along this same line that there is no intelligence in matter, is to declare that there is no intelligence in the laws of matter. But a law in order to be a law must express a certain phase of intelligence. If there were no intelligent expression in matter your body would be vapor one moment and possibly a soap bubble the next; your clothes would be a solid one day and a liquid the next; and what might nourish the system at one meal might decompose or consume the system at another meal. If there were no intelligent expression in matter the entire physical universe would be in perpetual chaos, and none of us could stay long enough in any one state of existence, to convey to each other the precious information that we did not exist. The very fact, therefore, that the books that claim to teach that matter has neither intelligence nor existence—the very fact that those books continue to exist in the same form proves that matter does exist and that the laws of matter do have intelligence.

The whole truth in this connection is that the entire universe is teeming with intelligence. Every physical atom is a center of intellectual activity. And every person who enters into harmony with this sea of intelligence will develop the most brilliant mentality and comprehend the greatest wisdom and the highest truth.

That spirit is real and matter unreal is another belief that the perfect understanding of truth will eliminate completely. Both are real, but we cannot discern the reality of either unless we view them on their own planes of existence. The mind that lives solely in physical consciousness cannot understand those elements and forces and states of being that are above physical consciousness. But every person can develop the consciousness that does understand what is above and beyond mere things.

To deny the reality of matter is to place one's self in that state of mind where it becomes impossible to understand the purpose of this present state of existence. However, we are here for a purpose, and if we do not fulfill that purpose now our present life will be for nought. But no one can go on toward the greater until he has finished the lesser. It is necessary, therefore, to understand this tangible world if we wish to promote the purpose and the progress of life; but we cannot understand that which we believe to be unreal.

In like manner it is impossible to use and apply properly those powers that exist in nature so long as we affirm that there is neither power nor sensation in nature. If we continue in this belief we will pass through this sphere of existence in a sort of materialistic dream life, and our happiness will be limited, or it may seem to be an ecstasy resulting from an overwrought imagination. We may live in part because we understand in part, and the reason why we understand only in part is because we refused to recognize the whole. This method of living may give health and may satisfy some minds for a while, but it does not produce the greater, the larger and the richer life. And no one can really live who does not eternally press on toward higher, better and greater things.

10

IN REALITY EVERYTHING IS GOOD.

When all things are reduced to their last analysis they culminate in what may be termed fundamental reality. And this reality is found to be good m every sense of the term. There is no evil in the fundamental state of things. And as the fundamental state is the origin of all expression there can, strictly speaking, be no evil in any form of expression. The effect cannot be evil in any of its phases if the cause be absolutely good. That is, the effect cannot be evil but it may contain conditions which can have an evil effect upon man. In other words, the expression of things must necessarily be good since the fundamental reality from which all things proceed is good But this expression may contain states or conditions that are not real, and that which is not real is not good, which means it has no actual existence.

Fundamental reality is complete in its fundamental state, but the expression of reality in any of its stages is never absolutely complete. All expression proceeds from the one state of completeness, and every expression is on the way to another state of completeness, but while on the way it is not absolutely complete. That which is being expressed is good in itself because it is real, and all that is real is good. But the expression is not real all the way through; that is, it is not filled to completeness all the way through. The expression itself does not have what may be termed fullness. In other words, it does not contain all of the real that it can contain. An expression is fundamental fullness in a state of expansion, and therefore contains many vacuums, so to speak, or many empty states which are states of incompleteness.

While any state of being is filled with all the reality it can possibly contain it does not contain vacuums. It is absolutely full and complete in that particular state, but when that state begins to express itself it begins to expand. It seeks a larger sphere of existence, and until it has developed itself sufficiently to fill that larger state, its fullness will not be complete; that is, it will contain many empty states; and we shall find in all our study that this condition of emptiness that appears in every state of development, is the one cause of all such conditions as are called evil or undesirable.

Every expression contains undeveloped states, and these states are caused by the fact that every expression is in a state of development. To develop the capacity to fill a larger sphere of existence is the purpose of every expression and everything has this purpose. It is the natural tendency of the entire universe to advance. Therefore all reality either is in expression at any particular moment in time, or is about to seek that expression. This being true it is evident that there are undeveloped states, or states of incompleteness, in every field of action whatever the plane of that action may be.

Completeness exists only where action has not begun a new movement of expansion, or when that action has been finished, and thereby causes the new movement to have filled completely a new sphere of development. But every finished action will shortly be followed by another and a larger action, so that what we call completeness never continues for any length of time anywhere. Whenever a greater state of completeness has been reached preparations are made by the law of eternity, which acts everywhere, for the reaching of a still greater state, and this is natural.

All forms of life are seeking greater expression. They are created for that purpose, and it is to their interest to promote that purpose. But every expression, being in a state of development, must necessarily contain states of incompleteness, and these states have been called evil because they are the direct or indirect causes of all those conditions that are not agreeable in the experience of man. However, these very states of incompleteness are necessary to continuous development.

There could be no advancement whatever if completeness were permanent everywhere; but since it is the purpose of all life to advance, these states of incompleteness are a necessary part of the great universal plan. These states therefore cannot, strictly speaking, be called evil. In fact, they are in a certain sense good, for without them we could not reach the greater good nor realize any change whatever. The truth is the entire universe would be at a standstill or absolutely dead if these states of incompleteness were eliminated, the reason being that all forms of development must have state of incompleteness through which and in which to develop. No development can take place where everything is already complete.

This being true, these states ought not to produce anything in the life of man that is not agreeable. In other words, that which is necessary to his greater happiness should not produce unhappiness at any time; and that which is necessary to his realization of the greater good should not produce such conditions as do not appear to be good. From this conclusion we judge that there must be a definite reason why undesirable conditions come at all since the cause of those conditions is so highly beneficial. And we also judge that man himself

61

must be responsible. In brief, we naturally conclude that evil conditions do not come directly from states of in completeness, but from man's ignorance of how to relate himself to those states.

It has been demonstrated conclusively that an incomplete state does not produce pain in its original condition of completeness, but that the pain comes when the state of incompleteness is unnecessarily prolonged. To avoid pain, therefore, all that is necessary is to proceed at once to develop every state of incompleteness the very moment that state appears in consciousness. From this fact we realize that so long as every state of incompleteness is constantly advancing toward a higher degree of completeness it does not produce pain nor produce any undesirable condition whatever.

The fact is that the feeling of pain indicates that something is being retarded in its progress, and that we are holding ourselves back from something good that is in store. Pain therefore is a good friend and is in itself good. It comes with good intentions and aims to prompt us on toward greater good. It is a friend, however, that we would rather dispense with, and we can. It is possible for the purpose of pain to be carried out in every sense of the term and in every phase of life without anyone ever feeling pain.

The same is true concerning undesirable conditions in general. They simply indicate that something in the human system is being retarded in its progress. They are therefore good because they prompt us onward toward the greater good, the greater life and the greater joy. When we accept this view of things we shall not think of anything as evil. We shall think of all states of incompleteness as good because they are necessary to progress and actually are expressions of fundamental reality moving toward higher realizations of absolute reality. And in a certain sense all unpleasant conditions that come from retarding the progress of these states of incompleteness are also good because they tend to produce progress where progress has been retarded.

The purpose of pain is not only to prevent greater pain, but to teach man how to eliminate all pain. The same is true of all conditions called evil. They tend not only to prevent greater evils, but also tend to arouse in man the desire to remove all evil in every shape and form. It is therefore scientific to state that everything is good because everything, that is at all, is an expression of fundamental* reality, and fundamental reality is absolutely good.

When man begins to view all things in the light of this understanding he will realize the fact that all pain, all suffering, and all undesirable experiences come from retarded progress, and that he will need pain so long as he continues to retard his progress. But when he no longer retards his progress at any time he will no longer need pain to prompt him onward. He will live every moment for continuous advancement. And the more he lives in this manner the more desirable will his life become because he will constantly be rising toward a more perfect realization of a greater good and a higher truth.

11

CAUSING THE BEST TO HAPPEN.

A certain phase of modern optimism has fallen into the habit of saying that everything is for the best. Whatever comes or not, according to this idea, be it good or otherwise, the mind is consoled with the belief that it is all for the best. And although there is a pleasing side to this belief still the final result of it is not desirable. To live in the belief that anything is for the best is to get into the habit of becoming content with anything; and to become content with anything is to cease practically all efforts toward the attainment of the higher and the greater. Such an attitude will also cause the mind to admit everything that may enter its world, no matter how inferior it may be.

A great many people, however, think that if we live in the convictions that all is for the best, all things will work themselves out for the best, and there is some truth in this. But things will not work themselves out for the best unless we cause them to do their best; and before things will do their best we must do our best. But the doing of one's best requires more than a mere statement that all is for the best. No person is doing his best unless he is giving his entire life to the very highest goal that he can possibly imagine. And no person can cause things to do their best unless his desire for the best is so immensely strong that all things are drawn into the irresistible life current of that desire. The mere passive belief about all being for the best is powerless in causing things to work for the best. And besides, to think that all is now for the best is to blind the mind so that it cannot see the better.

The rising mind sees greater things in the upper regions of the mental world, and must therefore realize that things as they are in the present are not the best, for they all can even now be made much better. The ideals of the present should be realized in the present; at least we should grow constantly in that realization; but the fact that we have failed to get what we want does not prove that it is best for us not to have it. It usually proves that we are incompetent, or that we have been negligent and indifferent, or that we have permitted ourselves to drift with the uncertainties of things. Had we lived more wisely in the past and taken advantage of the opportunities that the past presented, we should not have to wait now for opportunities to do now, what we think we should have the privilege to do. It is not for the best that any good thing should be deferred if we are ready to appreciate it in the present. It is not for the best that anyone who desires the greater should have to wait for opportunities to attain the greater. If he has to wait, his own past negligence is usually to blame. However, there must be no regrets. To weep over past failures is to waste those very energies that are required in the promotion of our present attainments.

If there is something that you want to do now do not think that it is for the best that circumstances are against you now. Instead, live in the faith that those circumstances must change, that it is for the best that they should change, and that you have the power to begin that change now. Circumstances did not make themselves. You have either made them yourself or you have accepted them ready made from someone else. But what you have made you can remake, and what you have accepted you can reject. Therefore, whatever may be the cause of your present circumstances you have the power to change those circumstances according to your own desire and need.

Circumstances, conditions and things have no particular object in view. Their function is to serve in the promotion of the objects that man may have in view. But when man has no definite object in view his circumstances will drift here and there as they are influenced by the circumstances of other and stronger minds. The man that has no definite purpose in life will invariably drift with the aimless-ness of the conditions in which he may be placed. If he does not control things he will drift with things, and he never controls things unless his desire to reach a certain goal is so strong that all things will be drawn into the immense force of that desire.

Here is the secret of controlling circumstances, conditions and things. Do not exercise any domineering force over things, but make the force of your own purpose so immensely strong that all things in your world will come and act in harmony with that purpose. The law is that every circumstance will conform itself to the strongest force that may pass through that circumstance. And the circumstance in question will give up all its power to work for the same purpose for which this strongest force is working. Therefore all things in your world will work for you when you make the force of your purpose in life a great deal stronger than any other force that may exist in your world. And this you can easily do by turning all the energies of your being into your one leading purpose.

Through this practice you will cause yourself to be your best now, and you will give your best to what you may be doing now. And when you are your best and do your best now all things will happen for the best in your life at present. The best does not happen to you in the present unless you are your best. And you are your best only when the best in your nature is working for the best that you can find in your world.

When in the presence of confused circumstances do not become passive or inactive and do not let things take their natural course. Things can do nothing of value unless they are guided. Therefore to let them work themselves out is to let them scatter and work themselves into nothingness. The result will be, not the best that could come to you, but rather the worst. When in a place where you do not know where to turn do not give up and let matters take their course in the hope that everything will turn out all right. It will not turn out all right unless you take matters into your own hands and lead them into the right. At such times be more determined than ever before; picture your higher goal more distinctly and have more faith than you ever had. Be your best and resolve to turn all things to the very best account. Thus the best will happen because you have made the best happen.

When you fail to get what you wanted never say that it must be best for you not to have it. You have a right to have what you want, and it is for the best that you should get it when you want it. Your failure to get it comes because you fail to be all that you could be and do all that you could do. So long as you continue to be the lesser, or be less than you can be, you will get the lesser, and the lesser is not best, for it could be better.

The belief that what is to be will be is also thoroughly wrong. Only that will be in the life of man that he himself will cause to be. And man has the power not only to change causes but to create new and greater causes. True, he must follow the laws of life, but the capacities of those laws have no limit. Therefore there can be no end to the possibilities in him who applies those laws according to their largest possibility and measure.

There is no fixed time for life or death, and no events are pre-ordained. Every life can be prolonged. Every event could have been different. And everything that happens to man could have added far more to his life than it does. From this fact we judge that few things happen for the best because man himself is seldom at his best. Nearly everything could have been better; but if they are not now what they might be, if we had been what we could be, the wisest course is to turn them to the very best account, and in the future maintain the very highest standard that the mind can possibly construct. When every person takes his life into his own hands and lives that life so perfectly that the very best that can be done now is being done now, ever5rthing will happen for the best. And what is more, such a life will advance perpetually into the better.

To cause the best to happen at all times, the secret is to awaken the superior power within and to place the entire mind absolutely in the hands of that power. After this has been done all things will work together for good, the very best must positively come to pass and every seeming disappointment will be an open door to something better. That better, however, will not be realized if we permit ourselves to be disappointed, because every depressed feeling takes the mind down away from the hands of superior power and will not be in a position therefore to appropriate those better things that this superior power is about to produce.

When the new way of living has been entered into and all of the energies of being have been directed to work together for the promotion of some great purpose, disappointments will hardly appear anymore. But should they appear the fact must be faced with the conviction that our failure to realize what we try to secure, indicates positively that something of far greater worth is to be secured shortly instead. When this conviction is invariably adhered to, regardless of what appearances may indicate, the law will never fail to bring the greater good. However, to secure positive and continuous results from this law it is necessary to eliminate everything in life that is not in perfect accord with the real science of life. Those tendencies that retard progress must not be permitted to live and act after we have resolved to do that only which can produce the best The mind must live on the heights and the soul must live for that life that is revealed while the mind is on the heights. There must be no compromise with half-truths or beliefs that are untrue, whatever experience may think. Form your purpose clearly, definitely, and positively. Aim at the highest goal in view. Desire the very best and make that desire so immensely strong that all things in your life will be drawn irresistibly into the current of that desire. All things will thereby work for the best, and the best will always come to pass.

12

THE TRUTH ABOUT RIGHT AND WRONG.

Everything that promotes the welfare, the advancement and the growth of the individual is right. And everything that interferes with the welfare, the advancement and the growth of the individual is wrong. This is the only natural standard by which we can judge what is right and what is wrong. It is therefore the true standard, being based upon the nature, the principle and the purpose of life itself.

When we analyze life we find that all life is progressive. To live is to move forward, because the real living principle has but one ruling tendency, and that is the tendency to press on toward the higher, the larger and the greater.

We also find that all the laws of life are constructive. They are all created for the purpose of construction; therefore to be in harmony with the laws of life man must live, think and act constructively. When man does something that is not constructive he violates the laws of life, and this is wrong because the inherent purpose of life is interfered with.

Here we may ask why some of the laws of life appear to be destructive. We shall find upon closer examination that all such laws simply promote the process of reconstruction. And the lesser sometimes has to be removed or seemingly destroyed in order that the greater may be built up. Realizing this, we shall find that all the laws of life are, to all nature and purposes, purely constructive.

The average system of ethics defines wrong as violation of law, but as such systems do not find the inherent purpose of law their philosophies of conduct are always complex and frequently misleading. When we understand that the inherent purpose of every law is to build or promote advancement and progress we realize that the violation of the law consists simply in refusing to move forward; in consequence every act, physical or mental that in any way retards or prevents the steady growth of the individual is a wrong act. And conversely no act is wrong unless it retards or prevents the growth of the individual. Therefore if we wish to avoid that wrong and be absolutely right in every respect, we must determine which acts of mind or body are natural and constructive, and which ones are not. This, however, can be determined by a very simple method; that is, by a study of mental tendencies; and all tendencies spring from mental attitudes.

A mental tendency is the mind in definite concentrated motion; that is, the mind moving in a certain direction with a special object in view, although this object may be unconscious just as frequently as it is conscious. There are a number of mental tendencies that are in constant action without our being aware of their existence. So that in such cases, the objects in view have become subconscious though they were in the beginning wholly objective or conscious.

A mental attitude may be defined as the image of the mind facing that toward which it may wish to move. And here we must realize the great fact that the way we face life determines our attitude toward life; and also the way we face things or look upon things determines our attitude toward things. A mental attitude is the placing of the mind in a position ready to move, and the way the mind is placed determines where it is going to move. When a mental attitude begins to move it becomes a tendency. And when the tendency reaches its climax it becomes an act. Therefore to know precisely the nature and inevitable result of the act we must know the exact position of the mental attitude from which it originally sprung.

There are a great many mental attitudes in existence, almost as many as there are views of life, and they divide themselves into two distinct divisions, the first division being right and the second wrong.

The reason why the attitudes of the second division are wrong is because the acts that proceed from those attitudes retard advancement and growth, and interfere with the welfare of man.

The first division of mental attitudes produces what may be called ascending tendencies, while the second division produces descending tendencies. Ascending tendencies culminate in acts that are constructive. Descending tendencies culminate in acts that scatter force, waste energies, pervert mental states, retard progress and produce discord, confusion and disorder in general. Ascending tendencies promote construction because they follow the laws of life. Descending tendencies interfere with construction because they resist the laws of life, and the reason why is simple. The first division of mental attitudes produce ascending tendencies because those attitudes mentally face the higher and the larger. In other words, the mind looks up at the greater possibilities that are before us while those attitudes are in formation.

The second division of mental attitudes produces mental tendencies because those attitudes mentally face the lower and the smaller. In these attitudes the mind looks down and takes cognizance of the ordinary, the inferior and the mere surface of things. Growth is an upward process, a process of expansion and enlargement. Therefore no tendency of mind can promote growth unless it is ascending, and moves upward into the larger and the greater.

From this brief analysis we conclude that the secret of being right is to mentally face the higher, the larger, the superior, the limitless and the absolute at all times. When all the attitudes of the mind are attitudes of an upward look all the tendencies of the mind will be ascending tendencies; thus the entire process of thinking will move constantly toward superiority, and every act will be in harmony with absolute law. This is simply understood because growth, advancement and ascension are the inherent purposes of all law. Therefore every act that is an act of advancement, or the result of advancement, must be in harmony with all natural law.

To violate law, to go against law, or to retard the purpose of law, is wrong; but to work with law and to promote the purpose of law is right. And since all laws are constructive, that is, tending toward the larger and the superior, we must, in order to be in harmony with every law cause every thought, every word and every act to have a tendency to move toward the larger and the superior. Thoughts, words and acts are the results of tendencies and tendencies come from mental attitudes. Therefore our effort should not be to determine what thoughts, words and acts are constructive, but what mental attitudes produce such thoughts, words and acts that are constructive. But here a multitude have made mistakes. They have tried to think right thoughts, but they have not tried to create those mental attitudes which naturally produce right thoughts. They have tried to express absolute truth in all their words and have expressed the letter of truth, so to speak, but the spirit of truth has not been expressed. The fact is we cannot express the spirit of truth unless the mind feels truth, and it is only the mind that is ever ascending into more and more truth that actually feels the truth. This feeling of truth demands the ascending tendency, which in turn is the result of the upward look of mind. In consequence, the secret of giving expression to truth is to turn all the attitudes of mind toward the higher, the larger and the superior. When we judge conduct we should always ask what the intention was that promoted the act, because if the intention was good the tendency back of the intention must of necessity have been an ascending tendency. Therefore something good will come from that act even though on the surface it may appear to be a mistake. There are many intentions, however, that are thought to be good when they are not, and whether they are or not we can determine by looking for the object the intention has in view. If the object is greater welfare, not only to self, but to everybody concerned, the intention must be good and good will come from it.

To formulate a system of conduct that will be right, the principle upon which to work is that of perpetual advancement along all lines. The central purpose should be to change the mind completely so that everything that pertains to the mind will face the greater possibilities of life. To this end all the eyes of the mind should be turned upon the most perfect mental image of complete character that we can possibly conceive of, and every act should be expressed with the positive intention of building toward that ideal image.

When all the attitudes of the mind are facing the greater possibilities of life everything that we do will carry us forward toward those greater things that we have in view. In brief, all things will work together in promoting this purpose to reach the greater things, and we will reach some of them every day. When the attitudes of the mind are turned toward the ideal, the perfect and the larger life, all things in life will turn the same way, because the mental attitudes determine how all other things in life are to be.

When everything in life is ascending toward the higher and the greater, everything will be right because to be right is to follow the laws of life, or to act as these laws act; that is, to promote the purpose that is inherent in every law. And that purpose is growth, advancement and ascension. In this study the great principle to be born in mind is, that so long as we are advancing along all lines we are obeying all the laws of life; we are not violating any of these laws and are therefore not doing anything wrong.

Another principle equally important is, that so long as all the attitudes of the mind are facing the greater possibilities of life, advancement along all lines will be promoted. The mind moves toward that part upon which its attention is directed. Therefore when the attention of every part of the mind is directed toward the greater possibilities of life every part of the mind will move toward those greater possibilities, and that constitutes advancement along all lines. Here we have the great secret of all development, physical, mental, moral and spiritual. When all the teachers of the world, whether they appear in the pulpit, the schoolroom or other halls of learning, will recognize these principles and apply them, we shall soon find a decided improvement in the human race.

When we understand these principles we see the folly of halt splitting arguments about what is right and what is wrong, and also the uselessness of trying to compel people to conform to artificial standards. Experience proves conclusively that those who are trying to live up to artificial standards of right and wrong are violating just as many laws as those who have no standards, but who simply are doing the best they know how. The cause for this is easily found. When a certain standard is fixed and you begin to pattern your life after such a standard your life will come to a standstill, and that in itself is a violation of all the laws of life. Even though the standard itself may be high, if your conception of that standard is fixed you will remain stationary by trying to live up to it. And the greatest wrong of all wrongs is to remain stationary; that is, to retard your own progress. We cannot obey the laws of life without moving forward, because as previously stated, the very principle of life itself is a perpetual forward movement; and so long as we move forward in all things and at all times we obey the laws of life without trying to do so. Therefore, instead of giving so much time trying to conform to all sorts of temporal laws we should give our time to the application of the principle of all law, which is growth, progress and ascension.

To obey consciously every law in our own sphere of existence is impossible. To simply enumerate them one after another would require an age. We realize therefore that in order to obey all the laws of life it is necessary to conform to the principle of all laws, which is advancement along all lines. When we apply the principle of advancement to everything we do, we will be in harmony with all laws without ever thinking about them. And it is this state which has been described as being above the law, or a law unto one's self.

This fact gives us a new thought with respect to the problem of wrong in the world. Hitherto we have tried to prevent people from doing wrong by literally permeating society with rules and regulations. But experience proves that this method does not reach the ills we seek to cure, and a study of the principles under consideration explains why. There is only one way to eliminate wrong in the world and that is to make it natural or second nature for man to do right. For so long as the tendencies of the mind are descending tendencies, wrong will be the result, and no number of regulations can prevent it. But make these tendencies ascending, and regulations will not be needed, because the inclinations of all minds will be to do right. We do not mean that man-made rules or laws should be done away with. Let society pass as many rules as desired, but there are two facts here that must be considered. One is, that the righteous man does not need the rules of man; and the other is, that the rules of man cannot reform the unrighteous. All that man-made laws can do is to protect society in a measure from the actions of the wrongdoer, but the wrongs themselves will continue as before.

Our object, however, is not simply to protect society, but to remove the cause of wrong in the human race; and to do this something else is needed besides the rules and regulations of society. The fact is that as soon as any mind begins real growth and progress all tendencies and desires to do wrong will disappear. This is perfectly natural because since growth is the normal purpose of every law you will by promoting your own growth naturally enter into perfect harmony with every law; and since there is absolutely no desire to violate law while we are in perfect harmony with law, all desire to do wrong will thereby disappear.

The man who advances along all lines naturally conforms with all laws, and he actually desires to conform with all laws because he has found that every law in life is a path to greater things. No man-made law therefore is necessary to prevent him from doing wrong. So long as he is advancing along all lines he cannot possibly have any desire to do wrong. Therefore if we would help mankind to do the right, and the right only, the secret is to teach every individual mind to promote the perpetual growth of his entire being, body, mind and-soul.

13

THE TRUTH ABOUT FREEDOM.

Freedom is largely a state of mind. It does not consist of the privilege to do as one pleases, nor does it mean deliverance from certain persons, environments or conditions. On the contrary, it is the consciousness of the fact that you have applied the truth as you understand it, and have lived according to your highest conception of eternal law. When you know that you have done right or have done your best you create a state of mind which to you, fulfills all the essentials of freedom, and in reality constitutes real freedom.

You are free when you are able to do what your present circumstances may require, and when you are able at the same time to rejoice in the privilege of such doing. The free man feels equal to all occasions and never dislikes what he is called upon to do, the reason being that freedom means not only emancipation from limitations, but also emancipation from any feeling of dislike toward anything whatever.

That person who believes freedom to mean the liberty to do as he pleases is in almost complete bondage, because when he is called upon to do what does not please, he either rebels or proceeds unwillingly, and there is no freedom in such a state of existence. Nothing, however, displeases the free man. He feels able to do everything with joy, and that is one reason why he is free.

The man who does what he pleases, or who tries to do what he pleases is on the down grade. He is following the desires of his physical nature, and those desires when left uncontrolled invariably lead to trouble and pain. But to be free we should follow the leadings of the soul and the desires of our higher and finer nature. The soul never asks to be pleased, but finds its greatest pleasure in constantly searching for opportunities to please others. The soul is constructed in this manner; therefore it is only by following the soul that we can find real freedom. The happiest and the freest man in the world is the one who never thinks of satisfying self, but who lives, thinks and acts according to the law of truth, and for the benefit of every living creature.

When you live simply to please yourself your consciousness becomes absorbed in the personal ego, and is therefore separated more and more from everything and everybody. The result is that your life is not only isolated from its higher source, but also becomes smaller and smaller until finally it does not seem to be worth living. When you follow the laws of life regardless of present personal desires you place yourself in harmony with the source of everything that is necessary to the welfare of the person. So that by a seeming personal sacrifice at first you enter into a larger life and come into possession of all that body, mind and soul may now require.

The world believes that the greatest joy comes from satisfying the desires of the person, and that freedom means to be so situated that one can always fulfill the wants of the present without being interfered with. But on this subject the world is wholly wrong. To follow the desires of the person is to enter hopeless confusion and ceaseless trouble and pain, the reason being that the person was made to serve and not to lead or rule. When the mind follows the soul and does what the soul may desire to have done, then it is that the larger, fuller life begins, and this life continues to grow and develop until the limitless is attained.

Here it must be remembered that whatever comes into one's life the person will receive, and also that the person has nothing to give, but is created to serve only as a receiving instrument. We realize therefore that if we continue to depend exclusively upon the person we finally come to a place where we depend upon nothing, and in consequence receive nothing. On the other hand, when the person is trained to give free and full expression to the life that is unfolded from within, and the mind is trained to enlarge its scope constantly so as to gain possession of a larger and a larger measure of life from within, the superior mind within is not only developed, but all the true desires of the person will be supplied.

We all realize that real personal satisfaction must inevitably follow the continuous expression of higher and superior states of being. But such expressions cannot take place until we follow absolutely the desires of our higher and finer nature, that is, the soul. The soul is the master, being the real individual you. The mind is the creator of the soul's ideals; and the function of the person is to receive and express in practical life what the mind creates. This is the law of life, and to live in harmony with this law is to attain perfect freedom.

There are thousands in the world today who can say that they have enjoyed perfect personal satisfaction for months or even years by following constantly the leadings and desires of the soul. These people did not do what they pleased to do in a personal sense, they did rather what the finer life within them sought to have done. And they found that in this way the higher pleasures were given to the person, while to mind and soul came visions of the endless paths and realizations of the life that goes upward and onward forever.

In our study of freedom it is highly important to understand that freedom never comes through a forceful separation from what we may call undesirable persons or environments. Freedom comes when we discover that these persons and things have a better side, and when we enter into conscious mental and spiritual unity with that better side. So long as you have the desire in your heart to separate yourself from anything, you are in bondage. The very fact that you desire separation from a person, an environment or a condition proves that you believe there is something evil in those things, and no one can be free so long as he recognizes evil or rebels against evil. Besides, the very fact you desire to separate yourself from anything that you consider undesirable proves that you are not above those things; and it is only the man who realizes he is above all conditions or things that is really free.

When you seek to unite more closely with the better side of what you previously disliked, the desire for separation will disappear, and the feeling of bondage will vanish. What is more, when you feel absolutely free, it is then that you are naturally and orderly separated from that which does not belong to you, and are thus transferred into the company of what is truly your own. When we do what is right and best because we want to, then we are free; but when we do not want to, we are in bondage to our own feelings or inclinations; that is, we are in bondage to ourselves. And he who is not free from himself is not free from anything. Briefly stated we enter that state of mind that we call freedom, when we can do properly and with pleasure what the present moment requires.

Order is heaven's first law. There is a time and place for everything, and everything is good when in its time and place. What we call evil is after all simply a misplacing of things. We produce evil when we do now what should have been done at another time or place. To use what is not ripe for use, or to neglect to use things before they are too ripe is to act at the wrong time and place. And such actions will produce adverse conditions. Neither the green apple nor the decayed apple are intended for the human system, but we partake of both when we try to live in the past or the future 1 instead of exclusively in the present. In like manner, when we use certain faculties or expressions where the law of order never intended that those things should be used, we misplace things. The result is confusion, and confusion always leads to bondage. To be in bondage is to have something in your way and when things are confused there are always some things in the way.

Freedom is a state wherein everything is in its true place and performing its true function; that is, a state wherein absolute order and perfect harmony of action prevails. However, the only way to have order is to follow the absolute law of life which is continuous advancement, or to live according to the truth and to do things as they ought to be done. But how are we to know these things? The person does not and cannot know; in fact, the average person is in a state of more or less confusion, and confusion is liable at any time to misdirect or misplace. Therefore it is not possible to learn to do these things properly by doing what the person pleases to have done. We all know too well that the guidance of mere personal desire leads to darkness, disorder and pain, the reason being that the person was not created to dictate to the mind. In consequence, whoever permits the person to rule or to lead, and who blindly follows the desires of the person, will invariably go wrong.

We shall know how to establish order and how to do things as they ought to be done when we know the truth, understand the principles of life, and follow the light of the soul at all times—never asking what we would like to do, but what is the best thing to do, because what is best we shall like the best when we find what it really is. And most important of all we should do with joy whatever the present moment may require. When we begin to follow the soul and begin to work toward higher and greater things we shall find that ever3rthing coming into life comes for a purpose, and also that the superior state of existence always follows when such purposes are fulfilled. Knowing this, we shall count it a privilege to do whatever comes our way.

We free ourselves from the disagreeable in life by placing ourselves in harmony with the better side of all things. And there is no better way to find the truer side of things than to meet all things in the spirit of a lofty rejoicing. To dislike anything that comes to us to be done is one of the greatest obstacles to freedom, because what we dislike we resist, and what we resist we place in our own way. What comes to us to be done we should work out. We cannot afford to shirk anything because what we neglect to do now we shall have to do later. In this connection we must realize that the only way to attain the higher is to work out of the lower; and this is a pleasure when done in harmony with the eternal order of things. However, if we wish to work out of present limitations into superior states we must follow the soul; that is, seek higher and higher realizations of the truth as viewed from the superior viewpoints of the soul, and do what the soul desires to have done.

To follow the person is to place ourselves in greater bondage to the limited than we ever were before because the person has nothing of its own. The person is only what we bring forth from within, and is large or small depending upon how much we express from our larger interior nature. But when we follow the soul and try to do what the soul may desire, we shall never fail to ascend into superior states of life because the soul is already in touch with the superior and the limitless. In like manner, absolute freedom must positively come when we follow the soul, because the soul lives and moves and has its being in that higher state of consciousness where absolute freedom is continuous, being the normal condition of that higher consciousness.

14

THE ROYAL PATH TO FREEDOM.

There are many when taken to task for not doing what propriety declares ought to be done, usually reply that they may do as they please with their own. They emphasize the statement, "What is ours, is ours," and we believe no one has the right to tell us what we should or should not do with our own. This form of logic may appear sound on the surface, or rather it may look good at a distance, but it changes completely upon closer acquaintance. The fact is that the idea, "We may do as we please with our own," is contrary to all true propriety, all principle, all science and all law. And whoever lives in the belief that he may do as he pleases will finally come to a place where he will not have the privilege to please to do anything. He will be in complete bondage to adverse circumstances which he himself has created, and absolutely at the mercy of a fate for which he alone is responsible.

When a person does as he pleases he usually follows the whims of fancy or obeys the commands of a per verse nature. He therefore disregards the real law of his being, and to disregard this law is to produce those very conditions that we do not want, and which do not please under any circumstance.

To do as you please in the general sense of that term is to produce that which does not please, while to act in accordance with natural law is to produce a perpetual increase of everything that is good and desirable, To do as you please with physical functions is to produce disease, because such actions will follow abnormal desire instead of natural law. To follow natural law, however, is not to go contrary to desire because normal desire and natural law are always in harmony. When the person is normal in all his tastes, appetites and tendencies every desire will desire to act according to natural law, and such desires when in action will not only promote construction and advancement, but will give the person far greater pleasure than the average person has ever known.

To do as you please with your mental powers is to weaken those powers, and to do as you please with your external possessions is to begin the downgrade to failure; because you will, when you do as you please, act contrary to the laws of accumulation and gain. In fact, no person can ever gain anything from any source so long as he uses things as he may please to use them. There is only one way to use anything, and that is according to law, because everything is subject to law; that is, natural law.

To disregard law in the use of anything is to step out of the world of law. And there is only one world that exists outside of the world of law, and that is the world of chaos. But to act in the world of chaos is to misdirect everything. In consequence we get only that which we do not desire or that which cannot possibly please in any sense of the term. When we act as we please we invariably follow the inclinations of the external person. But it is not the function of the external person to govern. The personality is but an instrument and was created to serve, It is the individuality that constitutes the real man; therefore it is the individuality that alone has the right to govern.

The normal attitude of the individuality, however, is not to do at any time what may seem to please the person at that particular time, but to act always in harmony with natural law, because it is such action that will in the long run please everything in the being of man. When the mind begins to do as it pleases it begins to drift, but so long as it follows natural law absolutely, it will advance toward greater power, greater wisdom and greater joy. It will gain ground constantly, and it will invariably reach the greater goal in view.

A fact of extreme importance in this connection is that the person who does as he pleases usually ignores the welfare of others and therefore tries consciously or unconsciously to live to himself, or to act to himself, which is not possible. To ignore the welfare of others is to place ourselves out of harmony with human life. And we can gain nothing of value from life when we are at variance with human life, because we are all dependent upon each other for what we receive in this world.

The man who ignores the welfare of the world will be ignored by the world because every action produces a reaction and the "select positions" he sought and gained will finally become a prison. To cut loose from the world in any manner or form is to create for ourselves a state of existence that can receive nothing of worth from the world. We will then not only be in a prison, so to speak, but that prison will be empty.

What man does to himself he does to the race. And what he fails to do to the race, the race will fail to do to him. Therefore no person can live to himself or act to himself. The part is invariably sustained by the whole, and is in consequence responsible to the whole. This is the law, but it is not a hard law. It is a law that governs every channel of supply or increase; therefore every individual who complies with this law will be supplied with ever3rthing that his life may require or need.

To violate this law constantly is to receive less and less until one receives practically nothing; and every person who does as he pleases invariably does violate this law. To live in harmony with this law is to receive more and more until one receives everything, and this is the destiny of him who does not do as he pleases, but rather pleases to do what his larger and finer nature has the power to do.

This conception of life does not in any way antagonize the principle of freedom because freedom is also based upon the same law. And it is a fact that there is no similarity whatever between the life of real freedom and the doing as one pleases. The man who does as he pleases is in bondage to his own misdirected nature, while that man alone is free who wants to do what his true nature declares he was created to do.

The purpose of life is to advance perpetually into the larger life, the greater life, the more beautiful life. And he alone is absolutely free whose whole life is devoted to the fullest possible promotion of that purpose. You are not free to do as you please, but you are free to become more and more and achieve more and more. And when you have learned to become and achieve more and more you shall find that it is such a mode of living alone that really does please.

To be free is not to have the privilege to follow any inclination that may happen along, because such actions lead to bondage, and we are not free to place ourselves in prison. For when the effect is bondage, the cause cannot be freedom. To be free is to have the power and the desire to follow the ascending, expanding, growing, developing, transcending tendency; that is, to break bounds continually and to rise perpetually in the scale of being, power and life. In brief, the free mind turns neither to the left nor to the right, but moves upward and onward eternally. The one purpose of such a mind is progress, and its ruling desire is to be all that is possible for a limitless mind to be.

To be free is not to have the privilege to anything you like regardless of whether those likes be normal or abnormal. To be free is to have the privilege to do that which leads to greater things; and than this there is nothing that could please us more. The man who does what he pleases will never be pleased with anything he has done, while the man who never pleases his personal self, but who gives his entire attention to his superior self, will be pleased with everything he has done. He will give a magic touch of high worth to every thought and to every act because he is living in the mental world of high worth. Besides, he is daily rising in the scale and will in consequence be more and more pleased with everything he may do or undertake.

There is no pleasure that is greater, no satisfaction that is more thorough, and no attainment that penetrates the soul more deeply than that which comes when we realize that we are steadily gaining ground. But to gain ground steadily we must transcend the present. We must grow out of the limited, we must live to be all that we can be. And it is such living that constitutes freedom. To gain freedom is to outgrow the present. To gain more freedom is to enter larger and larger mental domains, for the attitude of freedom is always a rising attitude. And when we learn this great fact we shall have found the royal path to freedom.

15

THE TRUTH BEYOND TRUTH.

There is something more in life besides that which appeals to the physical senses; there are other forces in the human personality besides those that are employed in muscular or chemical action; and there are faculties in the mind that far transcend the ones we usually employ in objective thought and reason. And since our purpose is to make the fullest and best use of everything that we may now possess, or later develop, nothing can be more important than to know what to do with those things that lie just beyond the limitations of the present, or to understand such truths as may be found beyond the truth we now understand. ,

The many are in the habit of declaring "one world at a time," meaning that they purpose to consider only what they are normally conscious of in the present. They refuse therefore to recognize what the senses do not seem to fully comprehend now. But in this connection we must remember that no step forward was ever taken without trying to transcend the ordinary and to picture the unknown. The very moment we resolve to consider only one world at a time, that is, only as much as present limitations can appreciate, we settle down in those limitations, and all advancement is brought to a standstill. Even in practical every-day life no progress is possible unless we try to go beyond the ordinary of the present; because in all things the greater lies before us and above us.

The truth we are now conscious of is only a small I fraction of the whole truth. An infinite sea of truth lies beyond our present consciousness, and it is our privilege to become conscious of more and more of this immensity as we advance in life. Therefore our purpose must be to try again and again to go beyond what we are conscious of now. All will admit that it is necessary in a certain sense to go out upon the seeming void in order to find the greater and the superior in reality. But the majority have placed an obstacle in their way as far as such an effort is concerned, though this obstacle exists wholly in their own minds.

That which lies beyond present ordinary mental action is frequently looked upon as supernatural or even abnormal. And it is simple to understand that no mind can gain control or possession of that which he looks upon as supernatural. And herein we find the obstacle to which we refer. To think of anything as supernatural is to place that particular thing so far beyond normal action that it cannot be attained through normal action. In other words we always place our own normal actions so far below those things that we think of as supernatural that an immense mental gulf is placed between the two. True, this gulf exists wholly in our own minds and is purely artificial, nevertheless, it tends to separate the normal actions of our minds from those higher things that we must of necessity realize and understand if we are to gain possession of a greater measure of truth than we now possess.

The fact is that when we think of anything as supernatural we tend to so belittle our present normal actions that the greater cannot be reached nor comprehended by the normal actions of the mind. Frequently the greater cannot even be discerned since we have pushed it so far off, so to speak, into the supernormal.

To state that the known is normal and the unknown supernormal or supernatural is to produce the same artificial gulf between the known and the unknown. And frequently this gulf is so wide that the unknown on the other side of consciousness continues to remain but a cloudy mist. In the meantime the normal mind continues to remain in the limitations of present ordinary knowledge. Consciousness does not expand, the mental faculties do not develop and the mentality itself does not transcend that sphere of consciousness in which we function at the present time.

Those who think of the unknown as supernatural must remember that all things have in their day been unknown, and even the most usual of all things in our environments are still unknown to millions. But nothing can be normal or natural and supernatural at the same time; and what is more, that which can be comprehended by the natural cannot be supernatural; in fact, it must have been natural all the time.

There was a time when classical music was unknown, but that does not prove that the classical is supernatural. There are thousands today who cannot appreciate classical music. It is beyond their reach. And though it is beyond the normal functionings of their minds, this fact does not prove that the music itself is supernormal or supernatural. Many have found classical music to be perfectly natural so that the power to appreciate such music is inherent in all minds; and therefore what some can appreciate in this connection all would appreciate sooner or later.

Nearly everything that is known today was at one time unknown and was looked upon by many as supernatural. But we have found all of these things to be perfectly natural, and we are fully justified in thinking that all things are normal and natural. To think of certain parts of life as supernatural is to form a wrong mental conception of those things, which will interfere with our better understanding of them, because men cannot gain a normal understanding of that which he thinks of as supernormal.

To state that all things are normal is simply to reaffirm the great statement that all things come from the same source, or that all parts are of one stupendous whole. And this is something we all believe now. There is not a person living that has not had, and that does not have experiences that are more or less beyond the ordinary. And a great deal of practical good might be obtained from such experiences if the qualities through which they are produced were more fully developed. But those faculties cannot be developed so long as they think of them as being out of the ordinary, as being special faculties, or as being supernatural functions of the mind.

To the average mind the supernatural means something that is beyond the present, something that the present cannot control, or something that is caused to transpire in the life of the person by some outside power or agency acting upon the person. But we cannot develop in ourselves that which we believe to exist outside or separate from ourselves. Nor can we learn to exercise a power which we think we do not possess. In the development of any faculty the first essential is to realize that that faculty is our own. And before any power can be mastered we must realize that that power exists in us and not apart from us. True, there are many minds who have extraordinary experiences even though they believe that those experiences come from supernatural sources, but it can easily be demonstrated that those very persons are highly developed along certain lines, and that they receive what they do because that development has taken place.

Those people, however, have no control over the faculties through which those experiences come. They cannot get what they want when it is wanted in this way, and they are more frequently misled than wisely guided by those things that are supposed to come in this helter-skelter fashion from higher sources. The reason for this is that no faculty, no matter how active it may be or how well developed it may seem to be, can serve us properly unless it is placed under our control. But to control a faculty we must know that it is our own.

When an impression comes to your mind that you ought to act thus or so and you obey that impression with profit, it is probable that you are informed by some outside agency since you were not conscious of exercising any special faculty yourself. Though it is also likely that that information came to you from your own subconscious mind. But if that information had been given to you by an outside agency you could not have received it if you had not developed that faculty through which it was received.

The gaining of that information therefore was wholly dependent upon your own mental development. We shall find that everything we gain, be it ordinary or extraordinary, comes through faculties of our own, no matter what the original source may be. And we must admit that we could receive a great deal more if those same faculties were highly developed. But we cannot develop those things that we look upon as supernatural, as being beyond us, or as being separated from us. Therefore to promote growth, development or attainment in any direction we must think of all things as natural and normal and as having the one Supreme Source. In like manner we must think of all truth as being expressions of the whole truth, and that higher truth is just as natural and intelligible as the truth we now understand. In brief, we must realize that that truth which may be beyond what we now know to be truth, is just as natural as the truth we now possess, and may be gained in the same way as we have gained such truth as we realize in the present.

There is a certain faculty usually termed interior insight that has become highly active in thousands of minds at the present time, and many of those who have it think that they are especially favored. They are sometimes warned from danger through mysterious premonitions and are frequently led into circumstances through which much good is gained. But in the last analysis can we say that a person who has a very active interior insight is favored to a greater degree than a person who has a good normal eyesight? Is not the one as wonderful as the other? Is not the one as natural as the other; and if it is true that mysterious warnings in the time of danger are supernatural, the ability to see the delicate colorings of the rainbow must also be supernatural. Though on the other hand if the latter is natural, as we know it to be, the former must also be natural, which fact proves that the sphere of the natural is infinitely more immense than we ever believed before.

To have a premonition of coming danger is wonderful, but to be able to see a broken plank in the sidewalk at a distance of one hundred feet is just as wonderful. Nevertheless, we have been in the habit of calling the one natural and the other supernatural. And for this reason we have pushed the former so far beyond us that we are hardly ever able to develop it further.

In this connection it is well to emphasize the fact that if we make it a practice to think of all extraordinary experiences as perfectly natural, we shall find it an easy matter to develop to a greater degree those faculties through which such experiences come. In consequence our minds would be enlarged along many new and interesting lines. Seeing and hearing and feeling have become so commonplace that we do not think of them as wonderful anymore, and yet to be able to see or hear or feel is just as marvelous as the most astonishing miracle that we ever heard of. In fact, to be able to predict events for a thousand years to come is no more wonderful than to be able to see physical objects a thousand feet in the distance.

This is something that we must realize if we wish to develop the mind along those higher lines through which greater truth may be discerned; because so long as we look upon certain things as extraordinary or supernatural we shall not be able to widen the mind into that consciousness through which such things may be realized or gained at will.

All things that are possible are wonderful—even extraordinary. Therefore if we should say that any one of them is caused by outside powers or agencies, or powers that are beyond us, we would have to say that they are all produced by such superior powers. Though if this were true man would be a mere automaton. To realize, however, on the contrary, that all these things, no matter how wonderful they may be, are being produced through faculties that belong to man, and that still more wonderful things can be produced through higher faculties already latent in man—this is to make man what he really is—a marvel of creative power.

To admit that some of these remarkable things take place through the actions of human faculties is to admit that more and greater things can take place through the further development of those same faculties and we know that this is true. Therefore we must conclude that every faculty is a marvelous faculty. For the same reason we must conclude that physical sight is just as wonderful and just as sacred as spiritual discernment; and also that the latter is just as natural and just as normal as the former.

If some things were sacred and some were not there would be two antagonistic causes in the universe, which is impossible, because a mind divided against itself cannot stand. The universe, however, has continued for ages and its laws and forces are still working together in harmony, invariably producing the same effects from the same causes, proving thereby that all things come from the one supreme source, and are governed by the one fundamental law.

Therefore if anything is natural, all things are natural since all things are produced by the one power. Also for the same reason all things must be sacred and good in their own place of action. And if one faculty in man belongs to man himself all faculties or powers that act in man must belong to man himself. The so-called higher faculties are parts of the human mind. They are not produced by special actions or by special powers outside of ourselves, but are caused to act by the same law that operates through all our faculties.

These faculties can be developed to higher and higher degrees just as every faculty in mind can be developed. However, to develop any faculty we must become conscious of the greater life and the greater possibilities that lie back of and above that faculty. But if we think of the greater life as being supernatural we at once imagine that it is beyond us. In consequence, the normal mind being lowered, cannot go up within reach of this greater life, but will hold itself back, so to speak, and thus be unable to promote the development desired along those lines.

But when we think of the greater life as being united with the lesser life, just as the inlet is united with the sea, we place the mind in that position where it can draw upon the greater life and thus increase constantly the power of every faculty. In like manner when we think of the limitless sea of infinite truth as being united with what truth we possess now, we place the mind in that position where it can gradually and steadily enter into the understanding of truth that is beyond what is understood now. And it is in this way that the mind goes into the realization of higher and greater truth along all lines, thereby fulfilling the one purpose of every mind in search of truth; that is, to become conscious of a wider and a higher world of truth every day. When we know that the higher faculties may be developed by the same power through which any development is promoted, that power will enter such higher faculties as we may wish to develop. The result will be that everything that now seems supernatural will be placed under the full normal control of the mind. And the dawn of the limitless life, as well as the understanding of infinite truth, will be at hand.

16

DISCERNMENT OF ABSOLUTE TRUTH.

It is impossible to define absolute truth, as that which is absolute is beyond definition, containing* within itself the elements of all definitions that might be formulated with regard to the truth. But for practical purposes we can say that absolute truth is the real or the whole truth in its changeless condition without any colorings or modifications whatever from the mind of man. Therefore to discern absolute truth the human mind must transcend all relative and isolated viewpoints of truth, and look upon the whole truth as it is in its fundamental and unmodified state.

This, however, is not possible so long as the ordinary senses are depended upon exclusively, because the senses invariably take special or isolated viewpoints, not being able to see anything from all points of view. For this reason the senses do not see things as they are in themselves all around, so to speak, but see things only as they appear from certain viewpoints. What is discerned from these viewpoints, however, is true as far as it goes, but it is not the whole truth. It is not the pure light, but simply a certain shade or color of the light.

But the absolute truth is the pure light—all the rays of light and all the colors of those rays blended in the one complete light. And it is such light that we must search for when trying to discern absolute truth. For the term "absolute truth" means practically the same as the pure white light of the whole truth. However, as the external senses and the usual actions of the mind approach the truth from certain viewpoints only we shall not be able to discern absolute truth, the pure white light of truth, unless there is some faculty or sense in the human mind that is in possession of this particular power. But there is such a sense— well termed the metaphysical sense—a finer sense in the human mind through which the absolute truth may be discerned.

It is the advent of modern metaphysics that has demonstrated the existence of a metaphysical sense, or rather a special mental faculty through which the whole truth about things, and the perfect soul of things, may be discerned. And it is through this discovery of the metaphysical sense that practically all misunderstandings concerning the study of metaphysics may be thoroughly cleared up.

An instance of such misunderstanding is found in the fact that a number of minds find the principle of metaphysics very simple; in brief, so simple that no mental effort whatever is required to understand them. While on the other hand a large number are unable to see anything of worth in those principles.

When we compare the intelligence of those who appreciate metaphysics and those who do not we usually find very little difference. There are many brilliant minds in both classes, and any number of lesser minds in both classes.

It is very evident that the principles of metaphysics are not discerned through the channels of ordinary objective intelligence. Neither does the understanding of metaphysics necessarily follow the higher development of character, because some of the best characters in the world are wholly unable to appreciate metaphysics, while there are a number who do appreciate such thought whose characters are by no means strong. And so marked is this difference between the two classes in this regard, that those who understand metaphysics are extremely surprised to find so many intelligent people seemingly unable to understand it. On the other hand, those who do not appreciate metaphysics are surprised to find so many believing in what to them appears to be nothing but illusions. Thus each party feels sorry for the lack of intelligence in the other, neither party knowing the cause of this particular difference.

The fact is that those who appreciate metaphysics do so not on account of any superiority in character or intelligence, but because they have the metaphysical sense developed to a considerable degree. On the other hand, those who do not fully appreciate metaphysics fail, not on account of any inferiority in character or intelligence, but because the metaphysical sense in them has not been developed. They may be very superior both in character and intellect, but if they have no development of the metaphysical sense, metaphysical principles will not be clear to them.

And here let us remember that metaphysics, properly defined, means the interior understanding of absolute truth. In brief, if you can discern what is usually spoken of as pure metaphysics you have the metaphysical sense, and have the power to discern, at least to some extent, the pure white light of absolute truth.

To criticize those who do not understand metaphysics, therefore, is not wisdom, for it is not their fault. Neither do we necessarily deserve any special credit for being able to understand metaphysical principles. Usually we are born with the metaphysical sense, and that is why metaphysical ideas are so simple to us. Why some are born with that sense and others not is a different question, however—a question that can readily be answered; but the answer has no direct bearing upon the subject under consideration.

The fact that the metaphysical sense is developed in some and not in others explains why some can appreciate metaphysics while others cannot. And the fact that the understanding of metaphysical principles is of extraordinary value leads us to enquire if the metaphysical sense can be developed in anybody here and now. The result of such inquiry and investigation proves that this sense can be developed. For the fact is that anything in the being of man can be developed. We all have the same powers and faculties latent within us, and the elements of growth are present in every faculty and power, so that it is only necessary to apply the law of development to that which we wish to develop and such development will invariably be secured.

The development of the metaphysical sense is important for many reasons, though there are two reasons that occupy the first place. The first reason is, that it is only through this sense that we can discern absolute truth, or pure truth, or the whole truth, in connection with anything in existence. And second, it is only through this sense that the mind can discern the causes of things. And here it is well to emphasize the fact that the world of cause exists entirely within the world of absolute truth. If man desires to master himself, take his life into his own hands and create his own destiny, he must understand the causes of the many effects in his life. And as causes can be discerned only through the metaphysical sense we realize its exceptional importance in this connection.

When man knows the cause of everything that takes place in his body, mind or character, and learns how to produce that cause he can produce practically any effect in his system that he may desire. If man knew the cause of health and knew how to produce that cause he could banish sickness from his life for all time. If he knew the cause of peace, harmony, wisdom and power he could in the same way produce those faculties or conditions in his life to any measure desired. The same would be true with regard to any other faculty or power that may exist in the being of man.

It is evident that when the metaphysical sense is highly developed we shall be able to know instantaneously the exact cause of everything that transpires in the human system. And this is perfectly natural, because if the physical sense can discern effects it is evident that the metaphysical sense can discern causes, functioning as it does in the world of cause. There are already thousands of people in the world who know that the causes of things can be discerned through the metaphysical sense, and who have had remarkable experiences in this connection, even though the development of this sense is as yet in its infancy.

We ourselves produce the causes of everything that happens in our own personalities or in our own world, though all such causes are as a rule produced ignorantly. The way we think and live will determine what is to happen to us. But the average person does not know what kind of thinking and living is necessary to produce the things desired. He knows desirable effects when he sees them, but he does not know what causes will produce those effects. And his ignorance in this regard is due to the fact that his metaphysical sense is not developed.

When the metaphysical sense is developed we shall be able to know the exact cause of every effect, and will therefore know what to do and what not to do in order to secure the results desired. The advantage of having a highly developed metaphysical sense therefore is extraordinary, to say the least, though its most important function will be found in connection with the discernment of absolute truth.

To develop this sense the principal essential is to train consciousness to go back of things, back of effects and into the world of underlying principles; that is, every mental effort should have cause in view, and every mental action should be animated with the realization that the principle that underlies every cause is not only ideal, but real; and that the real is perfect and complete, existing fundamentally in absolute truth.

To realize the completeness, the perfection and the wholeness of life, and the power that is back of things and within things, is also extremely important, because what we become conscious of in the interior life, that we shall invariably express in the exterior life. Through the metaphysical sense we discern the ideal, we realize the perfect, the greater and the complete. We become conscious of those elements in life that have superior quality and worth; and according to the law just stated we will thereby bring forth into tangible life the greater, the superior, the perfect and the ideal. Our ideals will thus be realized, and the remarkable possibilities that are latent within us will steadily unfold themselves into practical life.

To dwell mentally in the consciousness of the ideal, as far as that consciousness has been awakened, and to give constant attention to the discernment of the pure white light of absolute truth, is to aid remarkably in the development of the metaphysical sense. Here we must remember an important law; that is, that we tend to develop the power to discern and understand those things that we think of the most. Therefore, if we think a great deal of the pure white light of absolute truth, and try to enter into that light as far as possible, and as frequently as possible, the metaphysical sense will steadily develop.

Every action of consciousness that tries to feel the soul of things will produce the same effect; that is, tend to develop the mind toward the realization of the soul of reality, or absolute truth, and especially so if we think of the soul of things as being perfect and complete in every sense of the term; for the soul of things contains the whole truth that is in things and upon which the true existence of things is based. The workings of this law of consciousness, and the expression of what we become conscious of, is well illustrated in the fact that when the metaphysical sense discerns that the soul of things has perfect health, we thereby cause the mind to become conscious of perfect health. Perfect health, therefore, according to the law will become an active power in mind, which means that the power of health will fill the entire body. And this is true because the ruling power of the mind always becomes the ruling power of the body.

The metaphysical sense can also discern all other desirable qualities in the being of man. And since we always bring forth into expression whatever we become conscious of, a high development of the metaphysical sense will enable us to unfold and develop almost anything that we may desire, especially the full understanding of absolute truth. In addition, we shall know the cause of things, which means that we can determine the effect of all things in our world, thereby placing conditions, circumstances and destiny in our own hands. And this must be the inevitable result where the understanding of absolute truth is attained. For to know the truth is to be free, and to be free is to be able to make our own life and our own nature what we wish it to be. In brief, we are absolutely free when we have gained power to become and attain according to our deepest desires and highest ideals. And we approach absolute freedom as we grow in that power. The path of freedom is the path that leads upward and onward. And the further we advance in this path the more we discern and understand of the pure white light of absolute truth.

Made in the USA
San Bernardino, CA
30 August 2018